COMING INTO
ANIMAL PRESENCE

In this warm-spirited book of essays, John Lane's good-humored love for the natural world turns toward retrospection. Fossils—"talismans of time," he calls them; tales from collecting trips and field work; reminiscences of both texts and friendships that transcend the "shallow time" of daily life—Lane considers all these, sifting through more than four decades' worth of his deep love for the evolved, evolving world. Attentive to the wild and humane at heart, this is a lovely book.

—Elizabeth Dodd, author of
Prospect: Journeys & Landscapes

Part memoir, part travel log, part adventures in field biology, *Coming into Animal Presence* is a moving reflection on the roles of animals in human psychological and spiritual life. John Lane views the natural world through the eyes of a poet. He is a modern-day Henry Thoreau, and the swamps, woodlands, and rivers of the American South are his Walden Pond.

—Hal Herzog, author of *Some We Love,
Some We Hate, Some We Eat: Why It's So
Hard to Think Straight about Animals*

Coming into Animal Presence is the result of an attentive life spent in humility before creation—a storied meditation on presence among the many under-appreciated creatures with which we share existence. In a time when world weariness is the norm, John Lane reminds us of our unique gift as a species to join hands, fins, paws, and claws together.

—Brent Martin, author of *George Masa's Wild Vision*

ALSO BY JOHN LANE

POETRY COLLECTIONS
Anthropocene Blues
The Old Rob Poems
Abandoned Quarry: New & Selected Poems
Noble Trees (with photographers Mark Olencki & Mark Dennis)
Against Information and Other Poems
As the World Around Us Sleeps

PROSE
Still Upright & Headed Downstream
Whose Woods These Are
Seven Days on the Santee Delta (with Philip Wilkinson)
Neighborhood Hawks
Coyote Settles the South
Web of Water (with photographers Tom Blagdon, Clay Bolt, jon holliway, & Ben Geer Keys)
My Paddle to the Sea
The Best of the Kudzu Telegraph
Begin with Rock, End with Water
Circling Home
Chattooga
Waste Deep in Black Water
Weed Time

EDITED
Literary Dogs & Their South Carolina Writers (with Betsy Wakefield Teter)
Whose Woods These Are: New Nature Writing from the South (with Gerald Thurmond)
Hub City Christmas (with Betsy Wakefield Teter)
Hub City Anthology (with Betsy Wakefield Teter)

COMING INTO

ANIMAL PRESENCE

John Lane

MERCER UNIVERSITY PRESS

Macon, Georgia

MUP/ P660

© 2023 by Mercer University Press
Published by Mercer University Press
1501 Mercer University Drive
Macon, Georgia 31207
All rights reserved

27 26 25 24 23   5 4 3 2 1

Books published by Mercer University Press are printed on
acid-free paper that meets the requirements of the
American National Standard for Information Sciences—
Permanence of Paper for Printed Library Materials.

Printed and bound in the United States.

This book is set in Adobe Caslon Pro.

Cover/jacket design by Burt&Burt.

ISBN   978-0-88146-871-1 (print)
ISBN   978-0-88146-872-4 (eBook)
Cataloging-in-Publication Data is available from the Li-
brary of Congress

Animals are parallel cultures. You need to consult and incorporate all the nonhuman cultures that are occupants of the place....Story is a bridge. Build a bridge between art and the landscape.

—Barry Lopez (in conversation, 2010)

MERCER UNIVERSITY PRESS

Endowed by

TOM WATSON BROWN
and
THE WATSON-BROWN FOUNDATION, INC.

In memory of

James Kilgo (1941–2002) &
Barry Lopez (1945–2020)

friends and mentors

Contents

Preface   xi

ONE   1
Chronophilia   3
Ant Farm   14
Encounters of an Animal Kind   27
James Dickey's Animals   38

TWO   43
Field Work: A Memory Suite   43

The Everglades (1977)   45
Belize (1979 and 1981)   50
Southwest Florida (1988)   54
Zimbabwe (2010)   71

THREE   75
The Bear in the Freezer   77
Newt Love   85
Throwing Stars   89
Concerning Turtles   93
Rare Birds   99

FOUR   115
Two Elegies   115

Wild God   117
Piedmont Dreams   133

Acknowledgments   139
About the Author   141

Preface

This book has been in the making for decades. The oldest pieces were written in the 1970s, though several were written only last year. As often happens, I did not see any of them fitting together until they did.

I often think in threes, and this is the third book in my animal trilogy. Looking over the table of contents, I see new material and concerns, but I also see the seeds of more sustained works I've published in the past. In 2016 I published *Coyote Settles the South*, a book length reflection on coyotes coming into my region, and then in 2019, *Neighborhood Hawks* appeared, an almanac in which I follow our resident raptors for a year. These were both sustained attempts to tell personal stories with animals in them. In *Coming into Animal Presence* there's even a glancing encounter with a red-shouldered hawk and, in another, a coyote lopes past, as if calling out for its story to be told.

The first piece in this collection considers fossils, religion, and deep time and it takes a reader back to the Pleistocene. The last two pieces are elegies to departed writers and friends, James Kilgo and Barry Lopez. There's a lot of territory in the space between—travel pieces, journals, and essays. There are plenty of places and lots of people packed into this short collection. As with most of my nonfiction, I'm often in the presence of field scientists and friends.

Of course, there are animal presences too: the fragmentary fossil mammoth on Edisto Island. Scarce parrots in the Abaco Islands. A genet in an old Zimbabwean gold mine. A Florida alligator at full gallop. A caged jaguar and a playful cougar in Belize. A goose on a piedmont pond too small for it. Box turtles on the road. A bear in a freezer.

I'm not a PhD trained animal studies scholar or a wildlife biologist. What you'll see, though, is that I am a naturalist and creative writer with an irreducible love of wild things, even, and often even more-so, if they're in my own backyard.

John Lane
August 2022

One

Along with the other animals, the stones, the trees, and the clouds, we ourselves are characters within a huge story that is visibly unfolding all around us...

—David Abram

Chronophilia

On the surface, eight-year-old Olivia McConnell's request didn't seem that radical. The young South Carolinian asked her legislature to adopt the Columbian mammoth as the state fossil. South Carolina has many certified state symbols—folk dance, amphibian, animal, beverage, butterfly, color, gemstone, and onward, alphabetically, through over fifty categories. But South Carolina is only one of nine states without a state fossil. Olivia explained in her letter to the legislature that she wanted the mammoth because she read that a fossil tooth of the extinct elephant was discovered in a South Carolina swamp by enslaved people in 1725, one of the earliest of such discoveries.

Once the request was formalized into a bill, a state senator filibustered against it for several hours before concluding: "I thought we had passed a bill in the Senate putting a moratorium on official state whatever.... There's got to be a stopping point." Another South Carolina senator tried unsuccessfully to insert three verses from the King James version of the book of Genesis:

> And God said, Let the earth bring forth the living creature after his kind, cattle, and creeping thing, and beast of the earth after his kind: and it was so. And God made the beast of the earth after his kind, and cattle after their kind, and everything that creepeth upon the earth after his kind: and God saw that it was good. And God saw everything that

he had made, and, behold, it was very good. And the evening and the morning were the sixth day.

When that change was considered inappropriate, a new amendment was adopted. The mammoth would be deemed "as created on the sixth day with the beasts of the field."

"I think it's an appropriate time to acknowledge the creator," one senator added. "Since we're dealing with the fossil of the woolly mammoth, then this amendment would deal with the beginning of the woolly mammoth," yet another senator said, arguing for the amendment. After months of debate, the bill finally passed without the religious language. Finally, in May of 2014, the Columbian mammoth—not the wooly mammoth—became the official state fossil of South Carolina.

When I encountered the mammoth discussion, I knew I had stumbled into a debate in which I had an intellectual stake. I am a believer in deep time, and by the legislature trying to deny my state a fossil, I knew I had brushed up against willful ignorance, which I had been successfully purged of during my college years. In 1976, with my friend David Scott, I had walked the deserted Edisto Island winter beach in low-country South Carolina for a month every low tide and picked up fossils. One of us would take the lead for a tide, the other falling back submissively for secondary beachcombing. I don't remember much of what motivated me. That was forty years ago. It wasn't the grade I would receive—pass/fail/honors—for an independent January course. I could claim, it was the competition with David. He was both companion and rival, an academic star at the college, and one of the smartest of my friends. My freshman year I had earned all Cs. I could compete with David on the beach, though. Maybe it was the lure of the hunt. I had taken an intro anthropology course and knew modern humans had been hunters and gatherers for hundreds of thousands of years. My eye for pattern was just as developed as his, and I seemed to have a knack for identifying the fragments once we had them in hand.

David had a deeper scientific knowledge than I, for he was also a biology major, but together we both had this geology course in common and learned, among many things, of Scottish geologist James Hutton's discovery of deep time in the eighteenth century, of an assurance that our universe had "no vestige of a beginning—no prospect of an end."

Though my declared majors were religion and English, the geology class had created a deep fascination about time in me. You could say I was falling in love and about to become time's suitor. Our college's only geology professor, the proprietor of a one-man department, was named John Harrington. Harrington had left a university job training industry geologists to teach liberal arts majors how "to see a world." He told us about what he called "the wasness of the is" and illustrated the idea with the story of an Egyptian obelisk in Central Park. The monument was carved out of reddish granite about 1450 BCE. In 22 BCE, the stone was floated up the Nile and erected at Heliopolis. Fourteen centuries later it was moved to Alexandria. In 1880, the Egyptian government presented the monument to the people of the United States, and it was shipped to New York City, where, in 1975, it had stood for almost one hundred years.

Harrington pointed out that desert winds had sand-blasted the hieroglyphs. At some point, the obelisk had fallen over. If you knew where and how to look, he stressed, you could see how this one granite obelisk encompassed "half the earth, hundreds of millions of years before man's entrance on the stage, the full span of civilization, and [ended] in the back yard of the Metropolitan Museum of Art."

But Harrington also reminded us undergrads there was more to the story, and it was a story anyone could read. The rock's origin is Ordovician or Silurian, maybe as much as 410 million years ago. The tourist in Central Park, he reminded us, could not see the vast stretch of time it took to form granite, but it was possible for it all to be there before them anyway: "If he knows the language even this small sample [the obelisk] has a great deal more to tell."

One of the quickest ways to gain insight, for John Harrington, was to open this door of time. Once, Harrington was collecting rocks on the coast of England, and he found an ancient ax-head, and he imagined the paleo-Brit who made the ax so clearly that he was transported in time. "Separation in time was all that kept us from sharing my peanuts and raisins and well as some of our thoughts about the world and its ways," he told us when talking about that moment. Late in his life he began trying to put everything together and he began asking the vexing question, "How does the world work?" He'd ask it to strangers on busses, to colleagues in the lunchroom, and the best answer he got was from a Scottish doctor on a ferry crossing to Ireland: "It's simple. The world operates on a continuum between curiosity and fear."

Like the fundamentalists more than ninety years earlier at the Scopes Monkey Trial, some South Carolina politicians still believe evolution shouldn't be taught as scientific fact in public schools. They worry that natural selection doesn't explain what they call "the whole progression from microbes to humans," as if they believe evolution is a single thing, a fact. They say evolution should be taught as a pro and con.

Thinking this problem through, I found myself in deep intellectual water, dancing on the heads of several scholarly pins, both biological and theological. Read one way, this tempest in a political teapot over the state fossil might make some think ignorance covers South Carolina like a shallow sea, but one religion professor friend I talked with pointed out we really have nothing to fear from the fundamentalists. "What's heating up the planet is not fundamentalism. It's capitalism's willful ignorance. They're the dangerous ones. Capitalism as it's practiced in the world today measures time quarterly. That's all that matters. We used to say in the '60s, live for today and don't worry about tomorrow. Nobody wise lives that way."

Believe it or not, there have been some archipelagos of sanity in our state. A. C. Moore taught biology at the University of South Carolina in the early 1900s until his premature death in 1930. The herbarium at USC is named for him, as is a garden on campus. There has been recent interest in Moore's scientific research. "The *Spirogenesis* of *Pallavacinia*" is his contribution to meiosis cell-division research. He taught Darwin. In a letter to his wife, written on July 25, 1925, around the time of the Scopes Trial, he wrote:

> I fear the fundamentalists agitation has gone too far and harm will be done. Mr. Bryan has set going forces that he knew not of and that I fear will do incalculable harm. Unless the leaders of the church awake to the gravity of the situation and stop this effort to legislate men into the straight and narrow path, I fear the pendulum is going to swing in the opposite direction and that Mr. Bryan's prediction that this is going to be a battle between Evolution and the Bible will come true to the hurt of the Bible at least for a time 'til religious leaders come to their senses. What the churches should be doing is to encourage in every way the study of science to find out what is true and what is false and when truth is discovered to make it fit in with religious conceptions. It is no less criminal for a man to denounce the findings of science when he knows nothing about it and glories in his ignorance.

Later in the same letter, Moore wrote:

> I have had a somewhat depressed feeling this afternoon. The thought has been haunting me, "What are you going to do with all this you have been learning? Are you going home and be satisfied to enjoy it yourself—merely have the satisfaction that you know more than you did—that you are fairly well up with certain branches of biology?" I know myself well enough to know that many of my good impulses end without fruition. Is that going to be the case this time? I hope not. I ought to be able to teach better, but I can't help feeling a heavy sense of responsibility to the youth who may come under

my influence, especially at this critical time of religious unrest.

Since A. C. Moore's time there are fewer fundamentalists and more people like him in South Carolina—massive numbers of them—who believe in God but also believe in evolution. Olivia's proposal suggests the natural curiosity of youth and its openness to change. The arguments in the legislation reflect not ignorance but fear—fear of change, fear of loss of power, fear of the outside forcing its hand down on local rule and order.

We elect state senators who act (and legislate) as if they are ignorant of 150 years of scientific research in the history of life, or "creation," if you'd rather call it that. Where does this leave Olivia and her fossil mammoth? Is it destructive to her intellectual life to point to a statehouse bill she proposed about fossils weighted down with a piggyback rider about the Bible attached as well? Or does that argument reflect how the world works, one step forward into curiosity, and then one step backward into fear?

I guess you could call what I went through on Edisto Island a conversion experience close to religious, a moment when I was struck down on the road to Damascus. I had been to the mountaintop, or the tide line, in this instance. There was mystery and drama in that moment, emotions that amplified the day-to-day realities of time-bound schoolwork or family drama or community obligations. "Follow me," Harrington had said to us forty years ago, and we loaded busses and went out to see the world.

When we prepared for our fossil interim, David and I collected bones of dead animals in the fields and woods. Studying these bones taught us we could compare the modern bones to ancient bones and deduce what the other unknown bones might be. Size alone could isolate out the elephant bones.

Some folks in middle age have knickknack shelves of ceramic angels, but I still have my Pleistocene fossils, collected decades ago walking that fossil-rich beach on Edisto Island. To this day, a bone bed (maybe in the old river delta) is exposed in offshore deposits to surprise foragers as each tide recedes.

Along with the bones of wild animals we would not be surprised to see roaming the low country today—a whitetail deer antler, an alligator scute—we also found fragments of many exotic species long gone from the Carolina scene. On my study shelves I have kept horse bones that never saw a pasture, bison vertebra, a peccary tooth, the bony plate from the back of a glyptodont, and, maybe my most prized possessions—a three-cusped molar from a small extinct mastodon, the enamel worn down from chewing a vanished flora, and the symphysis of a massive lower jawbone of a large elephant, possibly a mammoth.

Most of what we picked up we could sort and identify, but to classify some of our mineralized booty, we had to seek out professional help, and for this we spent a week at the end of the project in the back rooms of the Smithsonian in Washington. The researchers there were impressed that Southern college boys knew so much, and they helped us fill out our species list of vanished fossil creatures of South Carolina.

These objects—heavy, mineralized bone—have traveled with me since college. Books and these fossils may be the only objects to survive my many moves and all the sorting and discarding of material things that comes with age. In each study that I have set up to write, the symphysis of the jawbone has adorned a shelf and the mastodon molar has been used as a paperweight. It's a miracle that the mastodon tooth has survived. It is fragile, the dentine and enamel already exposed and fractured when I picked it up on the beach forty years ago, with one gash of missing surface on the right rear. The fragment of jawbone has become a favorite party favor. I often haul it out to quiz guests. "What could this possibly be?" No one has ever guessed right. Some guessed bone and others fossil, but no one has ever approached an explanation of its origin.

I've carried these fossils around for forty years because they are talismans of time. They are scraps of a once-living world always blanketed partially in mystery. These creatures lived thousands of years ago in what is now my home state and we can imagine their lives. They died, were buried, and were raised from the dead by my plucking them from the sand on Edisto Island. I can read their narratives much as John Harrington read the story of the obelisk in Central Park. In the forty years since I found them, we've come to understand so much about life and the universe. The minerals making up the cells of these dead mammals were once star stuff.

I had majored in religion because I had a hunger for mystery, though little stomach for institutions, churches in particular. Wofford College is Methodist, and so the lectures and discussions in religion classes were stoked by a healthy liberal arts skepticism for anything that smacked of fundamentalism and literalism. Many a student signed up for Religion 201 hoping to have his or her shallow faith underpinned, only to find after the first semester in a religion course that their shaky foundations could be washed away. The professors taught biblical narratives as stories, not attempts at history or science, but instead at meaning-making. We were told that stories like those in Genesis reside in the faith realm, not a literal realm, and so they did not contradict what science discovers.

But belief is a powerful tide, and it is often not controlled by the moon of reason. The Minister John Bachman once said of Darwinism, "It's probably true, but I can't believe it." As an English major, this was an easy transition for me. I read widely and developed a love of stories and fell quickly victim to the idea that even the creation's story could be long and dynamic and that geology and ideas could give me a good set of Cliff Notes to help read it and even write my own chapters.

South Carolinians may suffer more from an ignorance of time than we do malnutrition, but there is a readily available cure: an education in natural history. I grieve the loneliness of the undereducated, living in their prison of shallow time. I mourn their belief in the poverty of time and its short fuse. I wish they could have taken a historical geology course. They would understand how, as John Harrington liked to illustrate with a line from William Blake, that it's possible to "see a world in a grain of sand, and eternity in an hour." One course in geology and maybe those senators would have stopped their bickering, but then again, maybe not, because their resistance is political, and politics is often erosion-resistant; throwing your support behind science doesn't often garner many votes.

Decades after my geology classes cured me of

common focus only on shallow time, I am still curious about the evolutionary processes. I see myself as one human being in a long line of my species—ten thousand generations standing side by side—back even through our original link to the primates, with their minions of ancestors, and even all the way back to the first bacterium and the big bang.

This love for time is the underpinning of my love of the natural world. I love the rocks because their certainty is dense and reliable. I love the forests because the clock of their days runs on sunlight and water. I love the rivers and streams because their flow is filtered through millions of moments. The animals? Each of us is a fuse set to expire in some sudden moment, even you.

Ant Farm

In the spring of 1980, my girlfriend said, "My biology textbook calls your poetry nothing but hormones and enzymes." Of course, the book was Edward O. Wilson's *Sociobiology*, published five years earlier, and the exchange
was a romantic shot across the bow of a potential mate. I
was hurt but I tried not to show it. I'd never heard of Wilson, so I didn't consider what he had to say in a biology
textbook particularly important on the subject of poetry.
After all, in 1980, we were just a few decades past C. P.
Snow's idea of "The Two Cultures," and I was clearly on
the side of what Snow called "the literary intellectuals."

I went straight to the library, though, and discovered
Wilson was known as "the ant man." More interestingly,
he was Southern, like me. He'd grown up a Baptist in Alabama. His love of the natural world started early. As a
child, he'd been the first to describe the introduction of
fire ants on Mobile Bay. Then he'd gone on to Harvard
for graduate school and figured out that ants communicate
by secreting a number of small chemicals called pheromones. As part of his research, he'd made a paste out of
ants and spread a sweep of ant calligraphy on a sheet of
plexiglass and watched the individual ants follow his trail.
This experiment was a major signpost for Wilson's celeb-
rity.

Ants are helpful, but they also enslave. They farm. They forage.
They also mine. In Arizona, ants find garnets and drag them

to the surface. Ants have existed for 130 million years. Phero-
mones can identify which nest an ant is from and also define
an ant's social status.

As a poet, I knew about pheromones, though I didn't call them that. I'd followed pheromones into several ill-fated relationships, like that one with my girlfriend. We argued all the time. She planned to go to medical school, and I wanted nothing but to write poems. As a poet, my evolutionary fitness was already in question.

When I finally read the first chapter of *Sociobiology*, I realized that Wilson had actually been talking about philosophers, not poets. Wilson points out that Albert Camus said the only serious philosophical question is suicide. But Wilson says Camus is wrong. "Self-knowledge is constrained and shaped by the emotional control centers in the hypothalamus and limbic systems. These centers flood the consciousness with all the emotions—hate, love, guilt, fear, and others." The most serious question, Wilson countered, is not why do humans kill themselves, but how do we survive? For Wilson, Darwin trumps Camus. The individual organism is a vehicle for the genes to reproduce, an "elaborate device" to spread and preserve our biological existence. The individual organism counts for almost nothing. Wilson had my attention right away. My father had committed suicide when I was four. So, it's easy to see why my girlfriend conflated/equivocated/reduced Wilson's ideas into a put-down of my life. The suicide father doubled down on my lack of reproductive fitness.

Once a queen has mated, her wings fall off. All of the workers in an ant colony are females. These females are all sterile. Male ants have wings and often fly in swarms in order to find mates.

But it wasn't always as easy to talk about my father as it is now. Until I went off to college, I lied about his suicide. I said, when asked, "He died of a heart attack," which I guess was true. The Southern novelist Walker Percy was an early fiction model for me—a writer who had also lost a father to suicide. Part of what I was looking for, unconsciously, was a method of dealing with the aftermath of the trauma of my father's death. Percy's novels were the pheromone that helped show me the way.

Wilson was shaped by a tough Southern childhood too. Wilson's father and mother divorced when he was eight. When the family fell apart, Wilson began to roam the fields and swamps of lower Alabama. "Animals and plants I could count on," he wrote in his memoir, *Naturalist.* There was also the trauma of losing an eye in a fishing accident and losing his Baptist faith in God. He's said that he felt no transcendence in church and "something small somewhere cracked."

Walker Percy's fiction was an odd choice for me. When I encountered it right after college, I was still essentially a poor Southern kid with little experience with polite middle-class or even upper-class Southern lifeways. Percy was an upper-class doctor/writer whose family had always had means. Affluence was another planet for me. In spite of our differences, there were at least two essential touchstones, though, with Percy—the suicide father and Percy's literary intersection with science.

Ants teach each other. Ants are able to navigate using the earth's magnetic field. Ants have a larger muscle-to-body ratio than humans. There are 12,000 species. They can carry fifty times their own body weight.

Science came to Walker Percy not through natural history, as it had for Wilson, but through medicine. Percy trained as a doctor but only practiced briefly. After medicine, he tended to ask philosophical questions about human nature and language in particular. First, he tried formal essays. Later, he stumbled upon novel writing as a way of crunching the data of human existence with both humor and irony. "My devotion to science is still with me," Percy said once in an interview. "I like its elegance and precision. As a novelist I'm interested in the same phenomena that I would be as a scientist."

I read Percy early and I've picked him up and reread his novels often. I love Binx Bolling in *The Moviegoer*, with his idea of "the search," and Percy's psychiatrist Thomas More in *Love in the Ruins* offering a living parallel and antedate to human fixation with apocalypse. In Percy's last novel, *The Thanatos Syndrome*, he returns to the rich character of Tom More and a situation where a future community is trying to social engineer the citizens by putting sodium isotope in the water supply. In this sort of plot there's a hint that Percy and Wilson were following the same literary pheromones—how to fix the world.

Percy also said that assertion is our primary cultural activity. It's one of the central acts of language. It's to be found in myth-making, storytelling, art, worship—and it's central to science. Percy described in essays and novels set mostly in the South, a world Wilson would have recognized from his childhood in Alabama. The fictional worlds Percy created endure on shelves and in libraries and in digital space. The characters he created cannot be reduced or summarized. They must be experienced as immediately as E. O. Wilson's fire ants.

Science, when it fails, tries hard to fit everything together too snugly, and if the world doesn't fit, it's reduced until it does. This reduction is one of the fundamental tools of science. Fiction, when it fails, loses touch with the particular nature of experience. Good characters run in fear of reduction. Good characters and good stories always open outward. They are specific data fields.

Some ants smell like rotten coconut. Some smell like lime.

So, as much as I admire E. O. Wilson, I struggle with his ideas about reduction. My girlfriend wanted to be a doctor, and she found it easy to reduce the thing that mattered most to me—my poetry—to hormones and enzymes. She found strength in that dismissal. Why does this still matter so much to me? My poetry survives. I survived. It's been forty-three years since she introduced me that day to Wilson, an introduction much more meaningful than a put-down. When I heard Wilson's name and one of his ideas, I began a search. Part of what I was looking for, unconsciously, was a method of dealing with the trauma born of damaging family patterns. Was this what my girlfriend was saying back then? Did she realize that poets will often follow the pheromone paths laid down by their ancestors? Was she worried I would I carry poisoned bait back to any potential nest we might build together?

Ants survived the ice ages. Ants were more resilient than dinosaurs. A prehistoric ant was discovered that had a wingspan of six inches.

I'll admit the 1980s was a fragile time. I was often melancholy and broke and hopelessly in love with the wrong women. Why didn't I commit suicide? One of the primary reasons I'd say is that I developed, like Wilson, a passion and love for the natural world, what Wilson called "The Creation." I loved rivers and mountains and found endless beauty and joy there. I even loved suburbs and cities, and because of natural historians and field scientists like Wilson, I learned to pay attention to the vast and endless gyrations of the universe. Wilson's example as a field scientist encouraged me to spend time with my own search—for wild animals from alligators to ants—and to see for myself what I shared with them. Why end your life when there is so much world to see?

When I finally read Wilson's *On Human Nature*, published three years after *Sociobiology*, I came upon this paragraph:

> I also do not envision scientific generalization as a substitute for art or anything more than a nourishing symbiont of art. The artist, including the creative writer, communicates his most personal experience and vision in a direct manner chosen to commit his audience emotionally to that perception. Science can hope to explain artists...but it is

not designed to transmit experience on a personal level.

Maybe Wilson would have chuckled knowingly about my reaction upon reading *Sociobiology*, and he perhaps would have admired how, after reading his work, I became a freedom fighter in his guerilla war against scientific ignorance.

But you never get over your discovery that a leading scientist believes you share so much in common with the ants, and that the thing at the center of your creative wheel is merely hormones and enzymes. I wish I had pushed harder against Wilson when my girlfriend first connected me to him. I wish I had quoted that great enzymic poet William Blake to her—"May God us keep/From Single Vision and Newton's Sleep." I wanted to be wide awake back then, and it seemed Wilson was shutting off the power to whole neighborhoods of human consciousness and boosting the signal to others.

I also learned a great deal from Walker Percy. I'm not a genius, but I believe, as Percy claimed, that genius is not about making great discoveries but in seeing the connections between the small ones. I'm always on a search and looking around.

The correct collective noun for a group of ants is a swarm. The sole purpose of a male ant is to mate. Once it has spread its seed, it dies. The average black garden ant has a lifespan longer than the average dog.

I began to teach environmental studies in the early 2000s, though my background to that point had been in creative writing and English literature. E. O. Wilson had become somebody, and by then I had been drawn to his popular science writing. I saw it as my pedagogical duty to the humanities to stake down the environmental studies tent, or, as I liked to explain it, to be the humanities leg of a three-legged stool, with science and the social sciences as the other legs.

Wilson would not have agreed with the stool metaphor. For Wilson, science was a language the whole universe spoke. It was the baseline, the common denominator. He believed the humanities put minds in a bunker, or, as he stated in his *Letters to a Young Scientist*, "However much the humanities enrich our lives, however infinitely they defend what it means to be human, they also limit thought to that which is human, and in this one important sense, they are trapped in a box." For Wilson, science wasn't a leg on the stool. It was the seat on which the human mind rested and worked in a systematic way to purify the method. By the time I began teaching environmental literature, I operated on a hybrid generator, finding metaphors in scientific research, turning the language on itself, expanding the reach of poetry into science.

At my college, our president and one of my colleagues conducted a seminar every spring. In the class, a group of outstanding seniors was invited to participate, and over the course of the semester, they conversed about a set of readings. Then, each year, they staged the Greek tragedy *Antigone* as their final project. I was invited to participate in the seminar and went to the play's final performance. The class used Seamus Heaney's version of the play, and the students really nailed it, memorizing their lines, using video and live performance, and there was not a trained thespian among them. In the seminar discussion afterward, the president guided the class in a deft examination of the characters of Creon and Antigone, the raw power of a despot versus the brave action of a single individual. When the president got around to asking me, the poet, about the play, I told the class that I kept thinking about Wilson and I kept seeing an ant farm—a whole species about its work, violent cycles on top of violent cycles over generations. I wasn't so interested in character as my friend the president. I was more interested in this relevance over eons. "We're a species a hundred thousand years past our prime," I joked to the class. "Maybe we don't have a tragic flaw. Maybe we have a species flaw."

My comment about the ant farm fell on deaf ears. The president wasn't interested in that path. He was an English professor by training and stayed with characters—the humanity of the play, the interaction of good and evil, the history of the staging, where it took place. It's not that I was opposed to that reading. Before encountering Wilson, I probably would have read the tragedy the same way. But by the time I'd entered the environmental studies department, I wanted to guide students in exploring the play through Wilson's eyes and see us as a species among species, ants among ants.

A colony of forty thousand ants is collectively as intelligent as a human being. Ants hear through vibrations. They have no lungs. They have tiny holes from which oxygen enters and carbon dioxide exits. An ant the size of a human could run as fast as a horse.

In 2003, I sat in an audience at Boston University and listened to the literary biographer Laura Walls chat with Wilson about his book *Consilience*, in which he tries to create a unified field theory of human nature, to bring together the sciences and humanities. Besides the reach and importance of his scientific research, by then he'd also won a Pulitzer Prize in general nonfiction writing. He'd written a memoir about growing up in Alabama. He'd even written a novel about ants. There was no literary landscape Wilson couldn't crawl and colonize. "We need to think like poets, work like bookkeepers, and write like journalists," he'd said that night to Walls. For an hour, Walls took Wilson to task, discussing science as a reductive form of knowledge. She spoke of science having "range and power" and literature "scope and beauty." She countered consilience with cosmos and confirmed that science's knowing was the anthesis of literature's feeling. "Literature cannot be reduced or abstracted," she asserted. I thought to myself, "Wilson. He doesn't get poetry at all. He conflates poets with philosophers." If I'd had the guts, I would have stood up that night and yelled some Roethke at him: "We think by feeling. What is there to know?"

The fastest animal in the world? An ant holds the record. An ant can survive a whole day underwater. The average fire ant sleeps around nine hours per day. The bite of a bulldog ant can kill a human in fifteen minutes. Ants can smell with their antenna. Each ant colony has its own special scent. This way, they can smell intruders.

I am no atheist, but I know there are atheists out there, and I welcome them to fling their arguments against the wall. I will respect their position as long as they don't descend into fundamentalism, the very force Wilson escaped in Alabama, the sort of black-and-white thinking that allows no opposition. I am an agnostic who believes in some loosely understood order and meaning to the known universe. I believe everything is in motion and that we humans are part of this universal swirl. I see all religious faiths as pointing in a rough human way toward this universal order and meaning, the way one might point toward the northern lights with a stick, with reverence and awe, without ever entirely understanding them.

Ants have two stomachs, one for their own food and one to feed others, that ants can go to war, and that ant blood is completely colorless. There is an ant colony in Southern California that spans six hundred miles.

In an interview in 2015 in *The New Scientist*, Wilson claimed, "What's dragging us down is religious faith. I would say that for the sake of human progress, the best thing we could possibly do would be to diminish, to the point of eliminating, religious faiths."

Wilson wasn't right. The consensus of science falls way short of this dismissive assessment of one of the cornerstones of human culture. I don't believe religious faith is dragging us down, and I don't believe anyone knows this in a scientific way, not even E. O. Wilson.

One of my friends, a Christian, said of this interview that it was one thing to dislike some category of other people, or to disagree with them. It was another thing—a second thing—to openly condemn other people because you disliked or disagreed with them. It was a third thing, he said, to advocate openly for their destruction and/or erasure.

If you placed all the humans in the world on one side of a scale and all the ants in the world on the other, they would balance.

When E. O. Wilson died at ninety-two, I was sad and conflicted. Every stunning revelation about the natural world—from ant pheromones to biogeography—and every thorny argument—from my girlfriend's put-down of my poetry to Wilson's quote in *New Science*—came rushing back. The situations and summations floated up and glowed in the final assessment of his achievement. What burned like phosphorous was the meme that was going around on Facebook about the time: "If you are not a scientist, and you disagree with scientists about science, it's actually not a disagreement. You're just wrong."

I disagree with some of Wilson's opinions. He privileged science over arts and humanities to the end, and my friend wasn't wrong when he pointed out that Wilson was calling for the erasure of religion. As they say in politics, I wonder if he ever regretted not walking that one back?

Where does that leave all of us who care for the work of E. O. Wilson? With a ragged shelf full of books, for one thing. Each contains a memory and example of his passion. Some of the books I will reread, like *Naturalist*. His science will continue to be tested because, as the meme suggests, science is not truth. Science is finding the truth. I won't have much to do with that. I am not a scientist. I am still a poet. Either controversial ideas such as the eusocial and group selection survive experimentation or they don't. Either way, it's no skin off Wilson's knuckles.

I'm with Wilson on the science, but I couldn't be with him as confidently when he stepped into the complex and unsettled world of human culture, which he did quite often as a "public intellectual." Where does most of Wilson's weight fall on the scale? One aspect of his last years was to work to preserve half the planet. Going into the future, this could be one of Wilson's best ideas, as important as any bit of research he contributed, as it would balance the scales for biodiversity, a kind of shared goal for poets and scientists, no matter the expertise.

Encounters of an Animal Kind

GOOSE ON THE POND

The first afternoon of the New Year, I came around the corner of the house and saw a full-grown Canada goose, alert but simply floating in the middle of the pond. I assumed it was a female based on her size. She watched me as I approached but made no attempt to flee. I thought instantly about the New Year's Day early morning's duck/goose hunt on our neighbor's nearby much larger pond. We have been, for almost twenty years, awakened at dawn as by a salvo of shotguns a few hundred yards up the creek. They must have hit her. I could see no visible wounds. I imagined she must have seen the tiny winking haven of our pond below and sat right down.

First of all, I called my brother-in-law. "It's just one of those country club birds. Kill it," he said, laughing. "I can use the meat."

"I don't think I can kill it," I said.

"Well, just leave it," he said. "There was a coyote in my yard this morning. Maybe it'll kill it."

Then I called a friend, a hunter. He assured me that if it wasn't spooked by my close approach, it was probably pretty badly hit. "Oh, I hate that," he said. "If they hit an organ it'll probably die. It's wounded animals like this that give hunters a bad name."

Then he told a coyote story. "A buddy was in a stand, and there was a little field in front of him surrounded by high-graded pines. He saw four coyotes come out of the tree line. Two just sat down and watched while the other two worked the field systematically. He knew if he was going to shoot them, he'd better go ahead, so he shot the two that were sitting. He said he was amazed they'd thought it all out, which two would sit and watch and which two would hunt."

As the afternoon progressed, I went about my business but kept an eye on the goose from the deck above as she floated on our little pond. She moved toward the edge of the pond little by little and was very aware each time we looked at her. I imagined just going down there, grabbing her, and cutting her throat. I love wild meat, and here I had a sitting goose on my little pond. I'd decided I was going to give the goose until the morning. I had a weird idea that if I left her overnight, she might bring in the coyotes I knew were in the floodplain.

This story seems so central now to what I've tried to convey about coyotes in the South. Their story is the same one as the dying goose.

As Aldo Leopold asks, how do we live in a world of wounds? How do we live in a world where everyone is not a hunter, and yet we buy our chicken from Publix? How do we live in a world with real neighbors who have no problem killing whatever flies through their airspace, lands on their ponds, or walks through their woods?

There were other wildlife encounters that week that seemed to swirl and merge with the goose and the coyotes: all week we had hundreds of vultures, black and turkey, soaring above our neighborhood. They'd taken up roosting in a line of oak trees three streets away. Once, on a beautiful late afternoon, I drove past, and there must have been a hundred vultures in the trees and another hundred soaring! I was sure my neighbors were freaking out, and yet every time they soared over our house, I got this great feeling of freedom, wildness, old patterns playing out. I kept wondering what was pulling them to that particular tree line. Was it some old homing instinct that goes back much deeper than our suburb? Was it the conjunction of thermals?

I've been watching crows and listening, too. I watched a *Nature* program called "A Murder of Crows" that outlined the complex communication among the birds and how they are probably the smartest of their order. I've been listening and watching.

I know I have very conscious and unconscious romantic notions about death and life and the wild that have been built in me through forty years of reading and experiencing, and I know I need to consider these ideas more deeply. I know there's a disconnect between the turkey meatballs our friends brought over last night for New Year's Eve and the lentil soup with a ham-stock base that I made the day before and my inability to kill the wounded goose. But do I need to abandon these feelings? Do they need rewiring? Do I need to become a killer to clear my soul just because I know I've entered into an agreement with corporate America to do my killing for me?

At dawn I walked out and found the goose dead next to the pond. It had been pretty cold overnight, but the goose was still warm. Her little black bead of an eye still seemed alive, the eye that had watched me the final day of her life. The body was stiff, even though the long elegant neck was still flexible. I picked her up and saw, finally, that her breast was speckled with little pink stains where the pellets had entered and found their mark. I oversentimentalized that dead goose. I held her to my chest and whispered like Timothy Treadwell to the wild grizzly in Werner Herzog's *Grizzly Man*, "I love you, I love you."

But what exactly was it that I loved? It was the idea of surviving wildness and how that goose and the coyotes and the crows and the vultures roosting in my neighbors' trees embody it, and it's also a longing for that thing missing in me. So, it's about absence and presence and how they are both the same. The reason I've wanted to write about coyotes in my suburb isn't to try and fill some emptiness entirely, some blank slate of understanding about them. It's also to understand me. I put the goose in the back of my truck, wrapped in a plastic bag. I took her over to my brother-in-law. As he said, he would cook it up and invite us over.

DIGITAL BIRDING

When I'd had my iPhone for a year or so, I often imagined how I might use it to increase my knowledge of one of my favorite subjects, natural history. I know it sounds like a contradiction in terms right out of James Cameron's *Avatar*—using technology to get closer to nature—but I've discovered it works.

There are dozens of "apps" (the small applications designed for use only with smart phones) whose purpose is purely old-fashioned natural history. Most of them are for identifying birds, though there are also apps for identification of tracks, scat (yes, that's what you think it is), fish, mammals, leaves, and the silhouettes of trees.

No self-respecting nature freak ever turned up their nose at binoculars. So, why not use an iPhone if there's some way it can really help learn a little more about nature? I first saw my phone's potential playing around with my new birding app on the back porch. Each screen within the program was dedicated to a different bird. It gave me a picture, a little text, and a recorded call. If I pressed an icon of a musical note a recorded bird sang its heart out from my tiny speaker.

I was surprised at first how loud it was. Although the sound came from a machine, not a real bird, the actual birds often showed up. The bird feeder was soon crowded, drawn in by the various songs I was testing out—cardinals, titmice, chickadees, even the nervous nuthatches. Then, a few weeks later, I was with a vertebrate field biology lab. The professor divided the students up into teams: one group would check the traps for small mammals to iden-tify, another would wade the creek and catch fish with a cast net, and yet another would make plaster casts of ani-mal tracks left in the sand the night before. The final group, two young women, would walk the trail with a field guide and identify their first birds of the semester.

I followed the novice birders and noticed right away the field guide they carried seemed unwieldy to them. They were of the digital tribe, I thought, and this book didn't seem quite right. They'd see a bird, try to look it up, and by the time they'd thumbed through the pages, it would be gone.

My iPhone provided a great teaching moment.

"Watch this," I said. I knew the birds they were watching were two female cardinals. I played their song, and they approached close enough for the young women to see them clearly and identify. The birds stayed around as I played the call over and over. I showed them the picture on the small screen, and the rest of the day they saw cardinals everywhere they went. And they knew their songs.

I'm not ready to give up printed field guides (I have dozens of them), but I saw that day that in the future, much of the identification we now do with books could probably be done with a phone. It won't be long before you'll be able to take a picture of a bird and the phone will identify the animal much quicker than you could open a traditional field guide—and then store the image in your own personal field guide. I can even imagine a time when all students in an environmental-studies class will be expected to have applications with bird calls on their phones. It will be part of their digital ecological literacy, one of the ways they interface daily with the natural world.

BIG SNAKE, SMALL MAN

Someone forwarded an e-mail my way with the heading "River Falls Rattler." The embedded picture showed a monster rattlesnake being held toward the camera on the tip of a stick. The body of the e-mail sounded official and stated that the snake had been found on a local golf course, warning golfers to be careful when retrieving balls from the rough. One glance showed the old bass fisherman's ploy of holding the creature close to the camera on a long stick, creating an optical illusion.

An e-mail back to the club confirmed the picture was a joke, an unappreciated digital hoax with the text doctored to fit whatever area it was circulating in. Joke or not, the golf course fielded phone calls all day—the speed of the internet and the fear of snakes is much deeper and more powerful than the logic of perspective.

The day before, I'd been talking with our dog sitter about rattlesnakes as well. She'd seen one dead about thirty miles west of our house, on the mountain front. I told her that was as close to Spartanburg as I'd ever heard of anyone seeing a timber rattlesnake, even though the range maps in all the snake books show them covering the whole Upstate. She was worried about walking the dogs. I assured her rattlers were rare and probably eradicated from our urbanized part of the county.

The next day, another friend pointed out a small article in a local weekly paper about a dead pygmy rattler near Lyman, a town only fifteen miles west. I could see his skin crawling with rattlesnake fear. He wanted to know how I could be so sure they weren't everywhere.

I told him I lean on science, my own observations, and the observations of my friends to believe such things. I'm one of those people who never passes a dead snake on a road without at least securing a quick ID. If there's any doubt about what's dead by the side of the road, I'll stop and check it out. I'm not saying they're aren't rattlesnakes where I live. I'm just saying I haven't seen them, and I'm always looking for them.

So, what is the real story with rattlers where I live?

South Carolina has its share of rattlers—huge eastern

diamondbacks along the coast that can grow to eight feet, the canebrake and timbers that can grow to six feet, and the two-foot pygmy, but after centuries of farming and development, these wilderness-loving creatures are now often few and far between.

Whitfield Gibbons is probably the leading snake man in the region. He's the coauthor of the beautiful field guide *Snakes of the Southeast,* full of great photos, range maps, and discussion of snake conservation. Besides being a University of Georgia professor, Whit's a tireless enthusiast for the wild South and the creatures that survive here. I e-mailed Whit and asked what he thought about the photograph of the rattler at River Falls.

"My first question would be—where did they find such a small man?"

And what about rattlesnakes in the Upstate? Are they here? He confirmed the range maps—even the ones in his book—show them covering the whole state.

"Their presence would not become apparent to most people," he said. "Except for ones crossing roads, most people (even me) can completely overlook a camouflaged rattlesnake."

He went on to tell a story from his own experience: "I just got back from Palmetto Bluff, where I have a student tracking seventeen rattlers with telemetry. Each of the four we sought out and found was coiled under a bush or log (one was even in the open on leaves) and I did not see a single one from ten feet away until the student finally pointed it out. And even when we moved within three feet of each one to take a body-temperature reading, not a single one rattled."

Whit concluded that a rattlesnake is a "fascinating animal that can only survive today when people don't know it's around."

So, this unexpected week of the rattlers is over. I'm sure they will come up again some time. Rattlers have too deep a hold on the American unconscious to go away completely.

CREATURES GREAT AND SMALL

I'm hoping this will be the spring we see river otters in the creek behind our house. I've had reports of people seeing them at the mill dam a half mile downstream, and just last week someone wrote to say they'd seen three otters fishing in Four-Mile Branch, a large tributary of Lawson's Fork not far away. There's something about a possible river-otter sighting that would fulfill my fauna longings for the season.

Otters are large semiaquatic mammals, three or four feet long, with blunt faces and thick necks and tails. Field guides report that they are intelligent and playful. They eat fish, crayfish, and mussels. Whatever's available in the stream, they'll eat it. Until a few years ago, they were considered in swift decline in piedmont streams. It seems they've been sighted more often recently, and though not abundant, they seem to have pushed back into former ranges.

I've often been skeptical when people report otters. Someone excited about a mammal swimming in a stream can easily mistake a beaver or a muskrat for an otter. The best way to know for sure is to watch closely for them diving and playing, and to check out their scat if you can find it. If scat is full of fish scales, it's likely left behind by an otter.

There's a funny term that I've heard used by wild-animal advocates: charismatic megafauna. Translated into plain English, it means large wild animals that excite the imagination. Usually, it refers to something bigger than an otter, something like that old list from *The Wizard of Oz*: "Lions and tigers and bears, oh my."

I think the human excitement over creatures large and wild is embedded deep in our genes. It's adaptive. In our shadowy past, we needed to avoid such encounters, because humans were part of the food chain and big fierce animals would eat us.

You know people still desire encounters with CM (charismatic megafauna) when you start hearing rumors of bear and cougar sightings. Even a large wild turkey sighted in an unexpected place can cross a local citizen into CM territory.

I once walked out of my building at Wofford College in downtown Spartanburg and found myself face-to-face with a large gobbler. That was a CM encounter if I've ever had one.

For some people, deer have built local CM appeal, which usually lasts until they start stripping your garden of charismatic mega and minor flora. Deer are so common now that they have somehow passed from wild and charismatic to a category that includes squirrels, blue jays, and crows—not quite domestic, but habituated to settlement so deeply that their presence usually doesn't excite our imaginations.

I think our excitement over smaller wild animals is something that's been developed in more recent times. The desire to interact with charismatic microfauna comes with the diminished expectations of the expanding urban areas. It takes practice and attention.

Here on the edge of the suburbs, I've seen how I've dropped my own expectations. Now, rather than mega-fauna, I look to the smaller creatures to excite my imagination. Often, I get excited about fauna even smaller than otters.

Two days ago, there were several wood ducks on the creek, and I flushed them on my morning walk. They shed a little charisma as they flew like bullets into the trees downstream and disappeared.

Last night, coming home on a rainy February evening, I saw the first gray tree frog of the season. The little frog with the oversized suction feet sat under the porch light waiting for a meal or for affection. It looked like it had been huddled under a log or a rock for a few months, all wrinkled and slow to move. But I can't deny it: that frog had charisma.

Charisma is the power to influence. All wild creatures great and small have it in abundance. If otters have returned to our piedmont streams, then it's more likely that someone like me will see them on a regular walk. There's no way to measure what such a sighting will add to someone's life, no way to predict what will change in them because of such brief encounters with wildness.

James Dickey's Animals

People who know my work and its association with James
Dickey—specifically, my 2004 book *Chattooga*—would
expect me to enter the discussion of his poetry at the landscape level: hunting and gathering examples of Dickey's
association with rivers, salt marshes, deer-woods, and
maybe that childhood tree house in the dark, cricket-buzz-
ing Southern suburban backyard. But it's on the level of
what I call animal presences that I want to enter this time,
to offer up a few observations about animals in Dickey's
work and how and why Dickey's encounters with and im-
aginings of animals are, I still think, particularly essential
and necessary today. *Presence* is from the Latin for "being
at hand" or "the fact of being present" or "a being, spiritual,
or incorporeal being felt as present."

   Animal presence, or animal being, is not unique to
Dickey's poetry, though I would argue he was one of the
best at it. It's what's found in Rilke's panther poem, in
Randall Jarrell's "The Woman at the Washington Zoo,"
in Elizabeth Bishop's "The Moose," in Mary Oliver's
"Wild Geese," in Ted Hughes's "Crow." In every example
here, when we encounter animal presence we are asked to
change. Maybe no American poet, with the exception of
Oliver, has such a roll call of animal presences. Maybe no
global poet outside of Hughes pushes the human mind so
far into that other order of presence.

John Lane

In Dickey's poems there are animals in so many titles, a menagerie, a wild and domestic kaleidoscope. I counted nineteen poems in *Poems 1957–1967*, most famously, of course, maybe "The Last Wolverine" and "Shark's Parlor," but also "The Heaven of Animals," "Listening to Fox-hounds," "The Sheep Child," "Encounters in Cage Country," and a dozen others. In the more expanded *Complete Poems*, edited by Ward Briggs, we encounter even more—in the index we find references to snakes, sharks, wolverines, crows, conchs, cobras, horses, eagles, foxes, trout, crabs, and buzzards.

If you followed all these titles back to their sources, you would encounter many examples of animal presence, but several of Dickey's friends have told me that some of the ideas for his animal poems came from watching early '60s Disney animal documentaries. From viewing these TV shows, Dickey was somehow able to tap into a deep understanding of prey-predator relationships exhibited in poems like "Heaven of Animals" and "The Last Wolverine." These insights didn't come as they did for someone like the British birder J. A. Baker, the author of *The Peregrine*, a book Dickey reviewed. Baker had spent ten years watching peregrines over the Essex marshes. Dickey's insights into animal presences seemed to come as flashes, and those flashes could occur in any sort of situation. Dickey's poems engender so many questions: he passed on his love of animals to his children. Is his daughter Bronwen's deep dive into the nature and culture of pit bulls an extension? His son Chris, the late Paris bureau chief of *Newsweek*, for years led a group of visiting college writing students on a pilgrimage to the caged presence of a

Gaboon viper that was the inspiration for "Encounters in Cage Country," and the plaque that marks the location of the poet's inspiration is still there for those interested in the influence of animal presences.

When I read Dickey's poems with animals in them, they make me ask a number of questions. It's the asking of these questions that is so important today, when the artificial line between other animals and Homo sapiens is blurring. One reason it is so important to stand in animal presence and feel it is that animals teach us to value the moment. It's all there really is—that one "wild and precise moment" that the late Mary Oliver talks about in a poem. Poetry helps us transgress the line between human and nonhuman—it helps us blur being—all the while understanding the clear differences. I can't be a bird although I might long to be. I can only watch and wish. Blurring means standing in common cause. It means understanding our common plight, the common cause of life.

But why do I think we even want to transgress? Does a bear ever want to be a bird? Is it our big social brains that give us this longing? We humans have evolutionarily sacrificed super-human traits. Why do our "superheroes" retain the abilities of wild things—to fly, superior strength, the ability to communicate beyond species?

We can never know what whales aspire to. When a whale surfaces and looks skyward with that big eye, does it aspire to fly? Why the stupendous leaps from ocean deep as if to do so? I don't want to be a whale, but I aspire to experience their world as they do, to somehow understand them in a way that blurs the lines between who we are—but at the same time defines the clear differences.

More and more, I am obsessed with this idea of common ancestors—we split with the plants 1.6 billion years ago yet still share one quarter our genes.

Does my beagle Murphy hear a coyote outside our yard howl and wonder who it is? Does he have dreams of running with this wild pack of recently diverged coyote cousins? With Murphy, our common ancestor is only sixty million years ago. I share 84 percent of DNA with Murphy. What does Murphy think of me?

I'd say that it's a safe bet to think that Dickey's work will be rediscovered by wider audiences again because of his animal poems. Poetry is one of the only ways we can cross the line. Books such as Franz de Waal's *Are We Smart Enough to Know How Smart Animals Are?* are particularly important to *inform*. But to *transform,* we need poetry.

Until that time we survive this fraught age, we need to ask and answer questions about the lines between us and animals we are willing to leave behind. We need to question our human exceptionalism. What is it to be present to animals? To the world they embody and are contained in? How do animals make us feel? What do animals mean, what do they mean to us? Can we become animal, or are we already animal? I feel at times that I just don't know how to properly think about it. I recently heard a podcast where the novelist Richard Powers, author of *The Overstory*, said that fiction must rediscover a "story" beyond the human. I think that poetry has never lost that recognition. The blurring. The merging. The "story beyond." Maybe the proper way to think of all of this is through poetry. Poetry and animals: the more we call their names and tell their stories, the closer kin we feel to them.

Two

Field Work: A Memory Suite

The way to do fieldwork is never to come up for air until it is all over.

—Margaret Mead

The Everglades (1977)

Along the edges of the Everglades National Park, cattle acreage and vegetable farms push up against wildness. "Sanctuary," Archie Carr called the park in his book *The Everglades*. "The Everglades are unique," he says. "They have no counterpart anywhere on earth." During my junior year in college, I spent part of a December and January in the Everglades on an independent study of subtropical ecology with my close friend David Scott. Cattle were far from our mind that December that we made our way south from South Carolina.

Professor "Ab" Abercrombie had agreed to be our sponsor for the class, and he told us what he knew of the Everglades, and let us borrow his old Grumman canoe, and sent us on our way. It's in the Everglades where I saw many endangered species the first time—the bald eagle, the reddish egret, the indigo snake, the Everglades kite.

The Everglades National Park is big—over a million acres—but most of the visitors stay on the few miles of paved roads and trails, camp in numbered spots in the campgrounds, and sleep in their Winnebagos. For us, our first month in the Glades was an outlaw trip. We felt that the regulations the Park Service had established were for the tourists who visited the Everglades, not us the young explorers.

We camped where we wanted, caught eight-foot endangered indigo snakes with our bare hands, photo-
graphed them, and then released them unharmed the next
day. We spent our days hip-deep in water and mud off the
trail, visited off-limits islands in the Grumman canoe.
Though Ab did not encourage our lawlessness (he wasn't
even aware of it at the time), he was like the threshold
guardian in the fairy tales, pointing the way down the
trails. He had told us to go and find wildlife in the Everglades, and that's we did.

David and I spent six weeks in the park that first winter, and it was there I encountered one of my holy places:
Buzzard's Roost. We were listening to an interpretive naturalist's program one day, and the speaker had called Buzzard's Roost a "paradise." I don't think she imagined that
there would be anyone in the tourist group who would actually hike through the saw grass to see the place, a full
mile off the edge of the trail. The next day, we walked out
the asphalt Anhinga Trail, past the railing separating curious tourists from the slough full of preening anhingas
and basking alligators. Just beyond this, one of the most
visited trails in any national park, we parted the button
bush and departed the well-worn trail. We walked a mile
through the saw grass on an old airboat track beaten down
by the park rangers on patrol and the park researchers
checking sites. The Everglades water was cool. Our long
pants and tennis shoes quickly soaked through to our
knees. The water smelled of rotting vegetation. Ahead, we
could see where the cypress trees formed a pyramid with
large old trees in the middle and stunted ones around the
edges of the circle of cypress.

We heard crickets and leopard frogs in the saw grass ahead of us. As we stopped once to listen, a ribbon snake at our feet was swallowing a frog. We took pictures and then noticed when we picked the snake up that it had been gorging on frogs! Its body was lumpy with them! When we let the snake go, it moved quickly through the saw grass in spite of its huge meal.

After a mile, the airboat trail veered off to the east, and so we followed an alligator trail the rest of the distance—about another mile—to the cypress head. The trail, really only an indention in the grass, led from a small willow head to Buzzard's Roost, and there were alligator tail drags and defecation all along the way.

Where we entered the dome a fringe of coco plum trees about fifteen feet high mixed in with stunted cypress, and the ground was matted with dead brown cypress needles. Inside the dome it was pure cypress and huge ferns: the old cypresses had fallen and were covered with them. There was a primordial feel to the place as the sun slanted through the shading branches. It was easy walking once we were inside, the cypress needles spongy under our shoes. David and I headed for the middle, where we could see water shimmering in the light gap. Egrets waded in the shallow water, and as we approached, two gators slid into the water. They were huge, over ten feet. We stood at the hole awhile, not saying anything. Finally, one of the shy gators surfaced, but quickly disappeared again under the dark water of the alligator hole.

Walking around the central alligator hole, David found a stinkpot turtle in the cypress needles and, a little further on, a green anole on a dead cypress. The way he caught the anole was pure David Scott: the lizard headed up the thin cypress, and David shook the trunk vigorously, whereupon the surprised lizard tumbled down from its fifteen-foot purchase into David's waiting hands.

A place like Buzzard's Roost would stun someone from the West, every inch of earth covered with a green maze of trees and grass that never stops growing and spreading, only slowing down a little with the seasons. Such a southern place, I've come to believe, is like the talk of Southerners, a snarl of connections and mannered greetings, a social history of words in every introduction, a verbal bramble in every square inch of space. The South Florida wilderness offers an annual growing season of more than 360 days. This single fact alone seems to separate the landscape from almost every other area of the country. That and the water.

I remember Buzzard's Roost now (it's been many years since I've been back there) as a shimmering place, a lingering, hidden, exposed, slow-flowing, duckweed-clogged stretch of water and trees. Three of the beasts that most sane people fear in the Everglades are there: rattlesnake, cottonmouth, alligator. They lay hidden, sunning in flattened pockets of saw grass. They move slowly from shade to shade. They catch and eat anything with calories.

At Buzzard's Roost, what started out as a simple interim class became something much more complex. It was the beginning of what would become for the three of us— Ab, David, and me—a sacred act, a yearly pilgrimage to South Florida, something very unacademic.

Ab joined us the next year, we canoed to Florida Bay's mangrove islands to look for nesting osprey, camped under

Australian pines, stared up at the wide South Florida sky, walked the Shark River trail, caught water snakes and baby alligators, then released them back into the canals.

We were beyond the rules and regulations that the world was living by, and we knew somehow how important this outlaw stance was for us. It was what would release us; the country needed wild and endangered species, but we needed wild and endangered experiences.

For David and me, these times were the tail end of childhood; we would soon graduate from college and have to face creating a living somehow, still not sure if we wanted "the real world," as our friends called everything beyond college, to pass us by. Looking back, those days in the Everglades were the formative acts that taught me that the experience I needed was out there on the edge of the known, beyond what could be regulated or improved.

Belize (1979 and 1981)

The closest I've ever been to deep wildness was probably the first trip I took to Belize in 1979. This was before Belize was discovered by adventure travel and developed by large-scale industrial agriculture. There were still vast stretches of interior rain forest, and it's said that Belize had more jaguars per square mile than any country in Central or South America.

I was working in Washington State at a small press. My former professor and friend Ab Abercrombie wrote and convinced me to fly back from the West Coast to accompany him, my college friend David, and some other friends to Central America to help with the crocodile research Ab had begun.

In Seattle, I sold my Datsun for quick cash (it was the middle of a gas crisis), flew back to South Carolina, and prepared for the trip to Belize. It proved a feast time, though the trip's pace was relentless. Ab had moved more deeply "hard science," and there was the possibility that if we gathered enough data on the Morelet's crocodile, a subspecies of *Crocodylus acutus*, the American crocodile, he could be awarded a large research grant for further study to return to Belize the next summer. At that point, my interest in wildlife was still vague; nineteenth-century "natural history" was as close as I could come to defining it. I spent the three weeks in Belize listening, watching, and learning the names of a hundred new plants and animals. Belize became another wild holy place, like Buzzard's Roost.

We spent a week in the "high bush" with a jaguar hunter Ab had met on a previous trip. The hunter had told Ab he knew where there were many crocodiles, so we loaded his surplus British army Land Rover and drove forty miles into the Belizean rain forest on an old logging road to a place called Gallon Jug.

Once, when we were finally miles from the nearest paved road, Badar, the hunter, stopped the Rover near a small creek. He cut the engine, and we sat for a moment and simply listened. The sounds of the forest were deep; they undulated toward us from the understory and canopy stretching unbroken toward Guatemala. Something screamed in the forest. Almost like a child's cry, but much older. It was the wildest moment of my life.

"Have you ever heard a jaguar before?" Badar asked, smiling as he nodded toward the sound slipping into the distance.

Hours later, when we arrived at the end of the logging trail after two flat tires and an eight-hour drive (to cover less than a hundred miles), we walked to the edge of a lagoon and found the dried skeletons of three dead crocodiles.

"Hunters have beaten us here," Ab said. He showed us how even with the carcass dried you could see where each animal had the valuable belly skin cut away.

That night we carried the canoe to the water's edge, then walked it out through thick marsh grass to deeper water in the distant center of the lagoon. There was limited room in the canoe, and I volunteered to wait until the second shift. While Badar was off hunting deer and Ab and the three others climbed in the canoe. I stood in the grass in waist-deep water and looked up at the stars. Gallon Jug was not untouched (do any such places exist?), but I knew I would add it to my list of wild places, and I hoped that I could become its pilgrim as well and return someday.

The next summer there was a second trip to Belize, this time with funding from the World Wildlife Fund. Ab had moved another year deeper into science. I spent the month with another friend traveling from village to village throughout Belize, searching for crocodile hunters so that we could gather information about the crocodile-skin trade in the small country. Ab, David, and several other people were off catching and tagging the crocodiles they could find, and we crossed paths only every six or seven days or so.

On that trip, I decided that even if I acquired a degree in wildlife biology or ecology, I couldn't be a scientist. I saw clearly into the middle of what scientific fieldwork really is about: long hours, exacting observation, constant movement.

After a month in-country, Belize was a blur of villages, crowded buses, and the faces and voices of the dozen crocodile hunters we were able to interview. Near the end of the trip, I wanted to go back to Gallon Jug to try to hear a jaguar again and to hear the howler monkeys at dawn, deep in the tropical forest, but Badar told us how a large American citrus company had bought ninety thousand acres surrounding Gallon Jug and planned to clear-cut it and plant orange and grapefruit trees "for the expanding US market." The cutting had already started, and the place we had camped was now a tangle of burning stumps. The wild spot no longer existed, except in the imagination and memory.

Southwest Florida (1988)

Soon after lunch, we headed down the road south, cruising slowly, skirting the eastern edge of the swamp, past what was called Tick Camp and Singletary Camp to where the sand road intersected with the east/west two-track called Hercules Grade. Although only May, it was Florida hot, and the air was heavy with humidity. We passed through a cooling grove of live oaks at the intersection and onto the open palmetto flats east of the swamp. There, we saw our first snake of the trip, a five-foot indigo. Blue-black and thick-bodied, the snake was slowly crossing the two-track in the hot noon sun, and Ab pulled the truck into the grass fast, jumped out, and picked the snake up. Indigos are known as "good tempered" snakes (they rarely bite), so people often kept them as pets before protection laws were passed. Snake hunting, along with loss of the dry, sandy habitat the snakes prefer, has diminished their populations in the state. Though it did not bite Ab, the big indigo did let loose with a load of musk, and the rest of the day I would remember the moment on the road when we had found it. The thick spicy odor of snake stayed on Ab's hands and filled the cab of the truck.

———

I had been catching snakes with Ab longer than I'd been catching alligators, and the indigo made me remember one of our trips to the Low Country of South Carolina. That's when I caught my first poisonous snake, a canebrake rattler. Ab and David Scott had been somewhere off ahead of me, and as I was walking alone in a smoking Jasper County stump field, my pillow case stuffed in my back pocket, my snake stick tapping passing trees like a blind man, I spotted the rattlesnake sunning near a stump hole. It looked dead, so still and beautiful in the spring sun: its pattern of freshly shed skin, crosshatched triangles, a dusky dark gray against a cream background. For a moment I thought of trying to catch it by myself, standing there in the pine distance, but instead I whistled Ab and David from somewhere on the horizon and squatted on my haunches, looking at the silent rattlesnake.

I watched the rattlesnake for five minutes. I was close enough to see a mosquito land just past the head (at the point of one lovely triangle) and get its fill of rattlesnake fluid, then wobble off on tiny wings into the nearby burnt pine needles.

Ab and David walked up through the trees, having heard my whistle. "Canebrake," Ab smiled as he spotted the snake. "It's all yours."

I knew what to do but I was fearful. Ab had told us that most of the snakebites among snake hunters come when pinning snakes and transferring them to the bags. I took out my pillowcase and handed it to David. He'd hold the bag open when I had the rattler in hand.

As I stepped closer, the snake "buzzed" for the first time. Out West, rattlers are called "buzz worms," and "buzz" describes what they sound like much more clearly than "rattle." A rattle suggests something loose, dry, child-like even, like a bag of bones or a baby's toy or a ceremonial gourd; buzz is tight and serious: a doorbell to a room you don't really want to enter.

As I approached, the rattler lifted its head off the last coil of thick body and poised quietly in the spring air. My heart took the express elevator to my feet.

"Go slow or it's headed for the hole," Ab said, watching my progress. "You've got it if you take your time."

It watched me, and its tongue, forked like they say, tested the air in front of it for fear or movement. I moved slowly to my right, getting within a stick's length of the poised arrow head.

I reached out slowly with the flat aluminum end of my snake stick, and it touched the broad head lightly. I slipped behind it a little, applying pressure, pushing the head out, using the solid ground beneath to support my pinning. My heart had found some door in my feet and left my body by this point. It was buried somewhere below me, in the sandy soil of Jasper County, South Carolina.

"It's yours," Ab said. "Lean down and grab on."

David stood ready with the bag. I leaned over.

"Bag it," Ab said.

I touched the snake just behind the jaws with my right hand, its skin dry and cool, my thumb to the right, my other four fingers to the left. I squeezed a little and lifted. The snake was heavy and calm, like deadweight, yet with the full droop of something alive and warm. I moved it slowly toward the bag and dropped it into the bottom, and David tied it up.

———

Back in Florida, Ab released the indigo snake back into the bush where it was headed, and for the next several hours we explored a series of ponds just north of Hercules Grade, beautiful spots near Curry Lake. It was there we saw a herd of whitetail deer moving through grass downwind of us, and they made me think what it must have been like to be a Seminole out on a hunt. They did not see us and were not in that poised awareness you usually see deer in. They were moving slowly through the grass, deliberately, and they looked almost noble.

Finally, when we saw a big alligator sunning next to a water hole, Ab said, "I'd like to bring my human ecology class to Curry Lake to show them how much energy is in the margins, not in the big stands of trees."

"Aren't the big trees where the most energy is?"

"There are all types of mature systems," Ab explained. "There are mature dynamic systems and mature stable systems. The name of the game is fixing sunlight." He pointed to the expanses of flag plants around the pond and then to the pond itself. I could see huge gar rolling in the shallows. There was so much life around us. I felt for a moment the way William Bartram must have felt in 1774, in the Southeast. Florida was still unsettled, only the players had changed a little.

But I had the feeling that maybe Ab was only half right. The name of the game was not only fixing sunlight, but placing human value where and how the sunlight was fixed. Was that our human game? Was that why we were there on the ranch? How to value all this? The answer for me, this day, was the gar rolling in the shallows, the indigo snake, the deer moving through the grass. Was it right that we survey them? Name them? Inventory? Can we let any-thing in the world simply be—land, wildlife, air, space—and assume that everyone else will do the same?

———

Not until late in the afternoon, as we drove up to Tucker's Grade to find the large shallow pond behind Field Thir-teen, did I begin to get an answer to all my questions. Eve-rywhere we went, we saw cows, mostly the specialty breeds—various Brahman crosses—that are tolerant of the high temperatures and various diseases of South Florida. Three miles down Tucker's Grade, we parked the pickup, retrieved our snake sticks, and set off north toward where we knew the pond would be. As we broke through scrub myrtle along a fence line, we heard the most miraculous thing, the low buzz of thousands of honeybees hovering above the surface of a green pond to the east, dipping one by one to drink.

Thoreau says in his journal, "Some incidents in my life have seemed far more allegorical than actual; they were so significant that they plainly served no other use." The bees were this for me.

Maybe I remember the bees so clearly because Ab and I separated soon after we saw the them. In mundane detail, we had simply found the big shallow pond beside Field Thirteen, and Ab explained how we needed to split up to survey it. But there was more to our split than that. It was as if this would be the split that would come clearly in the swamp four days later. It was as if I was finally finding my own way among the fields, fixing my own sunlight, finding my own watering hole, my own imagination.

The pond was long, with an oak island in the middle. Ab would walk east to check that end, I west, and we would meet at the island. I followed him through the perimeter, ringed with a thick stand of alligator flags, and as we broke through them, we saw hundreds of green tree frogs holding to the elongated green leaves. I picked a frog off. It looked like a Hollywood model for otherworldliness: too green to be real, distended Yoda eyes, and long E.T. limbs. It clung to my palm like a rock climber before I placed it back among the standing flags. "If we were here in summer after the rains have come, the sound would be deafening," Ab said.

Soon as we separated, I was on my own. There were very few times on that trip that I set off alone. We had work to do. Mostly we walked and talked together, but when I broke into the expanse of the shallow pond, it finally felt the way I remember it used to feel looking for snakes in college, on nobody's payroll. It was the rhythm I remember, this rambling. I think it's what Thoreau would call "sauntering." Even though I had a vague purpose, looking for alligators, there was freedom and surprise in my walking.

This was at the heart of the mystery: Are we always working for someone? Or is there any freedom from the economic questions? The bees were so beautiful dipping to the surface of the pond for moisture, yet bees are a metaphor for work and obedience. Tradition has it that the temples at Delphi were erected by bees, so the work sometimes leads to orphic teaching.

The surface of the big pond was covered with wire grass, waist deep, and though I could not see my feet, I could feel them in the cool water, and I knew that the water was slopping over the top of my basketball shoes. I pulled up one foot and saw that my shoe was covered with duckweed. It was the first time I had seen duckweed. I thought of a photo I had seen in *Natural History* of an alligator drifting in deep water, its exposed snout covered with duckweed.

Duckweed smells wet, reptilian. It's the way the Devonian period must have smelled. Most times the open water in a pond or swamp in South Florida is thick with it. If you look directly down at water that has drained out of a cypress swamp, it looks black under the green scum of the duckweed. The small leaves of the duckweed, when examined up close, are more like lace than scum. They are quite beautiful, really. They make you want to look down again and see what else you have missed. The clear water with the beautiful duckweed on it makes me wonder what other mistakes I've made, what else I've overlooked.

I stepped onto a trail beaten through the grass by alligators, with eight or ten inches of pond water exposed in long slices. That trail headed off toward the oak island, and I had the feeling that we'd see some alligators there.

I slowly crossed the alligator path, continuing out toward the center of the pond. The water didn't get any deeper, and I had not seen any alligators yet. If they were in the saw grass, they were sunning where I couldn't see them. There were more alligator interstates, though, a dozen trails all leading toward the oak island. I discovered one spot that looked like an alligator cloverleaf, a place where many of the trails came together, and decided I'd take the largest trail toward the island. I saw thick, bulbed piles of alligator scat in the matted grass where the trails came together.

I looked east. In the distance, I could see Ab near a willow stand. He was walking the margin of the pond, following a regular grid through the grass. I felt guilty for a moment, sauntering as I was, my eye not on the prize of the oak island, the established goal, so I turned toward the high ground. I began to be "systematic," to cut the field into "quadrants," and returned to the "survey."

The island goal was only fifty yards from me when I heard a rustling in the grass on a parallel path beside me, so I ran to cut off what I thought was a small gator and stepped in its path. Bearing down on me, at full speed, was a ten-foot alligator, "high-walking" up on all four legs.

"Jesus," I thought. "It's attacking me!"

Then I stepped off the interstate and it passed by, close enough to touch, and disappeared onto the island. Now my heart was covered with duckweed. I walked slowly toward the island looking from side to side.

When I reached the island, which sits high and dry above the pond, I saw where the gator was heading. There were three small pools ringed with alligator caves at the center of the island. The big gator was merely beating a retreat past me from his sunbathing spot in the grass. He had heard me coming, and I just happened to step in the way. Had he hit me, it would have been like stepping in front of a bus, a bus covered with duckweed, with big teeth.

I found a log in the middle of the island and sat down. In the distance, I could see that Ab was finally working his way toward the island from the east. I would wait on my log for him, surrounded by alligators in their caves, safe from everything, it seemed. The alligators were enjoying life on their island. There was a fence along the pond's edge that kept the cows from wading out and stomping on their caves, but nothing to stop men like me who, on rare occasions, waded through the duckweed to step in their way and bring the twentieth century rushing in.

———

When Ab finally reached the island, I told him of my encounter with the big alligator, and he smiled. He noted a big adult on his survey sheet ("Ten feet, you say?" he said, raising one eyebrow), along with several alligators he had seen.

It was getting late, and Ab wanted to drive into "The Land of the Hairy-Dicked Cows" while there was still daylight, so we left the land of the bees and alligator interstates and walked out to the truck. Ab wanted to stop along the way at Boyd's Head Bay, one of the few spots of open water we had seen from the air when we flew the ranch. It took a minute by Cessna to fly from the ranch's center north to Boyd's Head Bay, but it was a forty-minute ride in the Dodge. When we finally closed the last gate behind us on Tram Road Grade and turned north at Grub Road, we knew we were in the wildest corner of the ranch. Once or twice the Dodge spun dangerously toward the soft shoulders, where we would have been stuck for an hour until we could dig it out and jack the axle up enough to get clear of the sand had we ventured too close.

Ab's theory was that the cows became known as "hairy

dicks" as corruption of "heretics," or escapees, from the herd. He had the theory confirmed when Peter Matthiessen mentioned "heretic" cattle in his novel about the Everglades, *Killing Mr. Watson*. Wherever the name had originated, Curry's wild cattle had become creatures of great mythological significance for us, something to discuss and look forward to seeing, as we rode from cattle pond to cattle pond, checking for alligators.

As we had walked through the improved pastures that week, Curry's cows had considered us in resolute silence, occasionally breaking into a clumsy, bewildered trot. That was the most emotion I saw them exhibit. I had never thought much about cattle, though there are probably more cattle in Florida now than there were deer or bison back when William Bartram, the Philadelphia naturalist, made his swing through the territory in 1780. I had once thought, watching squirrels on a college campus, that they were creatures of long periods of busy horizontality punctuated by excited moments of verticality when something frightened them up a tree. The Babcock Ranch cows lacked the exciting existence of squirrels and spent their entire lives grazing, chewing, and fertilizing until finally they took the blow to the head, then accepted the cellophane packaging.

"I think Curry's just bored and tired of working cattle," Ab said as we drove through the last of the improved fields. "Look at a few cows, and you'll quickly see they aren't the most romantic beast, that's for sure."

We pictured the wild cows as different. They had broken through the fences and become the road warriors of the Babcock Ranch cattle, bovine guerrillas living in small bachelor herds out beyond the last gate, where the pastures were not improved, the water was inconsistent, and the native grasses fought the saw palmetto for a toehold in the Florida sand. We agreed we'd feel lucky if we saw them, though Curry had told us they roamed freely the northern quadrant, where there were no fences, from Carey's Corner to Hog Slough, from John's Camp to the Yearling Pasture.

The deep blond sand, something we had not encountered on the southern half of the ranch, made the land of the renegades a ragged, hard place for any animal to make a living. The flat landscape was mostly scrub palmetto and a few wiry live oak. Ab speculated that if a cougar happened to wander down from the Fakahatchee Strand, country like this was probably where you'd see it, crossing one of these sand roads after dark, matching wits with the outlaws.

I'd always wanted to see a cougar in the wild. One of the things that made South Florida seem like a small slice of an earlier American wilderness William Bartram might recognize was the presence of large predatory cats such as the Florida panther. One of thirty species of *Felis concolor*, they once ranged from Terra de Fuego north into Canada. Now, healthy populations of cougars—also called pumas, panthers, screamers, and mountain lions—are found only in deserts, mountains, rain forests, and other isolated places. The Florida panther is darker than cats in the western United States, and its tail is bent, forming a crook at the end. They are shy and rarely seen, even by biologists who study them. Because of this, signs rather than sightings are usually the way they are located and kept accountable to the wildlife biologists.

Two of the confirmed tracks were fifty miles east of the swamp and seventy-five miles southeast, so it would not be impossible for a cat to wander this far east.

In order that the animal might survive, the Florida Game and Freshwater Fish Commission established the Florida Panther Recovery Program. Through a research and management program, they hope to rescue the cats from the threat of extinction. It's an expensive program, and a trust fund helps pay for it. The fund provides help with determining habitat demands of the big cats and settling conflicts between panther survival and public use of habitat. Ab has said that even if someone did find a panther track or a deer kill on a ranch, there was a good chance the rancher would not report it, not wanting to draw any more "environmental" attention to his ranch. As Curry had made clear, habitat paperwork was already deep enough, and he wouldn't want to add endangered-species baggage to his ranch.

The only other time I had come close to seeing a Florida panther was in the Everglades in 1976, my junior year in college. David and I were driving south toward Flamingo one evening. We had just left Long Pine Key, the northern campground in the national park, and rounded a corner on the highway when we approached a Winnebago stopped on the side of the road. The driver flagged us down and said he had just seen a "big cat" cross the road. We were sure from his description—long tail and big size—that it was a panther. I had been only moments away from being one of the dozen or so people a year to see a panther in Florida.

My only intimate contact with big cats was in Belize in '79. David and I were staying with a hunter who took rich Americans into the bush to hunt jaguar. The man had intimate knowledge of the Belizean rain forest, so he would take us to look for crocodiles. He kept a young jaguar in a cage in the backyard and walked us out to the cage the first day. The bloodhounds that he kept for hunting—blueticks and black-and-tans—were in a cage just across the yard from the jaguar, and they howled when we approached. The hunter had found the cat when it was just a kitten after he had shot its mother. He explained how he would let the jaguar go and then set the dogs after it, pulling them off as soon as the cat was treed, and in this way he taught his young dogs to hunt. I walked up close to the jaguar's cage. This was not a zoo animal bored and settled into the rhythms of life in a cage. This was an animal that still remembered the forest, maybe even the way it had been captured. I could see it in its eyes. There was a terrible insult pooled like dark syrup behind the horizontal pupils. I approached a step closer, and the cat crouched and swatted at the bars with a huge spotted paw.

The hunter also had a Belizean cougar named Fritz which he kept as a pet. He explained how jaguars and cougars had quite different temperaments and how a cougar could become what he considered quite tame. The cat wore a collar and had run of the house. Fritz was still a "cub," though he had almost gained his adult size, weighing almost a hundred pounds. Two things happened during our stay that showed me the power of that tame cougar, much less that of the caged jaguar in the backyard. Once, David was playing with Fritz in the living room, tossing a ball to him and watching the big cat bat it around as a kitten would do. Then David went to the bathroom, but when he returned to the room, the cat still wanted to play. He was hiding behind the door when David returned and pounced on him, knocking him to the floor and giving him a little play bite behind the head. Do I remember correctly that David had long scratches where the cat had slid down his back. Later in the week, I left my lightweight down-filled sleeping bag unrolled while we went into the field for the day. When we returned that evening, Fritz was batting the flying feathers around the room like shuttlecocks.

Now, the eastern coast of North America, from Nova Scotia south to Florida, has mostly been cleared of big cats—except for a small swath of South Florida near where we were. But as long as there are fifteen or so panthers working the cypress heads and palmetto flats, the Florida wilderness will feel complete.

———

There were fewer ponds in that part of the ranch than in the rest, but Boyd's Head Bay was quite distinct, a cypress head standing above the surrounding palmetto flats. "There it is," I said, pointing off toward the east as we crawled up Grub Road.

We walked through the palmetto flats and flushed a family of feral pigs, a mother and ten piglets, and gave chase to them, but to no avail. The piglets scattered like a broken string of pearls as the mother squealed and tried to lead us into the loose sand and ground palmetto, where our footing wasn't particularly good. It must have been family day because fifty yards farther into the bush we flushed a mother armadillo and her three identical babies. We managed to catch two of the babies, and they looked exactly like the mother, who had slipped under an old live oak log. Armadillos look like armored footballs trailing a lead-colored tail. Though nearsighted, their eye problems don't keep them from moving like a halfback when cornered.

We released the two baby armadillos and continued toward Boyd's Head Bay. Soon we were walking through knee-high cypress, which looked like thin Christmas trees with brown needles, headed toward the taller cypress, where we hoped to find the water and maybe some alligators. As we approached the center of the cypress head, we could see a large pond surrounded by bright green grass. Then we saw them: the wild cows on the other side of the pond, belly deep in the water, grazing on water hyacinths. We squatted and watched them for a few moments. There were five of them, and they had not seen us yet. The renegades looked just like the cows in the improved pastures, but there was something different about their attitude as they grazed in the water in a small herd. When we stood up, they saw us and rumbled out of the pond into the cypress just beyond and were gone. We sat down on a down cypress and looked across the pond. The grass was so green it looked as if we were seeing it through a filtered lens. I didn't understand anything about this small cypress head, much less Babcock Ranch. All I knew at that moment was that it was one of the most beautiful spots I'd ever seen and nobody should be able to own it.

"Why can't we just assign a 'non-value' to a place like this?" I asked. "Why does every place have to be worth something in our capitalistic terms?"

"You've got four approaches you can take to the world: drop out, sign up and become a part of the system, revolt, or compromise," said Ab.

"That's it?"

"That's all I've seen work. They're all unacceptable to me, but there are no other options that I can think of."

"But what about the older system, the one the alligators and those cows are a part of? Why is everything in the world defined in terms of our system?"

"Because we can. Because we have. But you know that's not good enough for me either."

I watched a little breeze rippling the water, making waves in the grass. "Let's get to work," Ab smiled. We walked the edge of the pond and saw some tail drags of a big alligator, but no other signs. Later, we would fly over the pond in the plane and hope to see a big male sunning. That would be the only way we'd ever get back to Boyd's Head Bay.

We drove south, deeper in the land of the renegades. South Lighter Canal was dry, but we found a pond with a little water and some gators hiding along the edges. We watched a hawk for a while through Ab's glasses, sitting on a rotting pine top hanging out over the dry canal—a juvenile red-shouldered. He followed us as we walked the canal, would not leave us alone, kept landing in the pines, scree-screeing as we walked along. There were other birds, ground doves, nighthawks. There were more armadillos, escaping quickly into pine straw under the palmettoes.

Each stop confirmed for Ab what he had always known, that alligators are "creatures of great variability of habitat." There was an abundance of alligators in this side of the ranch, many with pods of yearlings, living in dry flag ponds and sloughs stomped down by the herds of cattle, but even there, in the dry sand, alligators were holding out in Boyd's Head Bay.

Walking back to the truck, we invented various conservation and research pipe dreams more plausible, in some ways, it was becoming clear to Ab, than a dream of ranching alligators. One thing was certain: the alligators of Babcock Ranch were survivors. Ab didn't figure we had to worry about them. We began to feel more sympathy for the cows living in the improved pastures, so we created a scheme to recreate the "wild cow," a super renegade. South Florida, Ab thought, would be perfect for it.

"This system was made for a big, wild herbivore." Ab laughed as he explained how he "would cut fertile cows by 90 percent, infertile animals 100 percent, and keep all the bulls. Then I'd introduce some exotic predator, maybe a hundred pregnant female coyotes, vaccinated for rabies and distemper, chosen from good southern Louisiana stock. And in a hundred years, the Babcock Ranch would have a mean, maybe even smart, wild cow."

Zimbabwe (2010)

Many years later, near the entrance to Africa University, we crossed the low end of a long, sharp north/south ridge that runs behind the campus. The ridge parallels the Mutare River, and we walked there along a trail with soapstone rubble left behind from local carvers. Then the trail starts to climb the ridge toward the top.

The river was hidden below us in the trees, and when we caught glimpses of it, the water was loaded with red silt, the byproduct of a Russian industrial gold-mining operation upstream. It's a small river, and the flow was loaded like a piedmont stream would look after a two-inch rain. It's terrible. I mentioned something to Ab, and he said, "Well, the Russians screwed up their own country, so why wouldn't they do it here?"

The walk was hot and dusty. There were sprigs of green in the trees but not much to announce spring. Ab said it was much greener than it was a week ago. The whole ridge had been burnt, and we could smell smoke in the air from a huge fire down the Mutare Valley. I was wearing Chaco sandals and my feet were black from the soot after a few hundred yards.

I was amazed by all the soapstone. I was used to seeing it in small outcrops, but the whole ridge was thick with it. Ab said that when they walked here after a rain, the trail was very slippery. We talked about how the soapstone industry of local craftsmen and artisans would make a great senior project for someone back at the college where we taught. It would be interesting to know how far back the practice went and who the masters were and whether or not it developed out of the tourist trade. There were also several ruins of structures on the walk that perhaps went back to colonial times. Lots of human artifacts on this walk too—one particular rusted-out machine left by gold miners was strewn over the hill side. Ab called it a "rolling mill," and picked up a heavy bearing that had been used to pulverize the ore.

From the ridge trail on the backside you could look across the river and see the next ridge line, which was the campus boundary. The views up valley and down were wonderful, though with winter's dry season the palette was a little limited—mostly browns and grays with surprises of green where the trees not in need of water leafed out.

One of the reasons Ab wanted to take the hike was to check some GPS points for a hike he needed to do the following week, so we were searching out a cave that Ab's wife, Chrissy, had found on one of her hikes. It was an old horizontal gold-mining shaft, and Ab said a genet lived in it, so he wanted to install a game camera there to see if they could get some pictures. I had never heard of a genet, so Ab explained how it was a small African cat with a long spotted body and a striped tail, like a racoon. He said that on a previous excursion he had found a large collection of genet scat about forty yards in, to the right, and that he actually saw the cat for a moment. The day of our hike, Ab handed me Chrissy's snake stick and a small flashlight. He told me to go in and see for myself. "I wouldn't go past the right turn. The cat still might be in there, and we don't want to scare it."

I started in and was surprised when a fear engulfed me. I used to do stuff like this with Ab all the time, but it had been years. I kept walking anyway and went in about ten yards and inched over a large pile of rock where there had been a small collapse of the ceiling. I looked back at the entrance, and then I look forward into the darkness. "Don't be stupid," I thought to myself. "Just go a little further. It's fun to challenge your fears like this. It's why you came to Africa." So, I shuffled forward a dozen more yards. I kept telling myself, "Just get a little farther and you can turn around. Go as far as you can."

The shaft was tall enough so that I could stand upright. The flashlight was small but it was bright. It illuminated the shaft but not for far. It was cool and dry in there. I kept looking at the ceiling because Ab had told me of some of the other shafts they'd been down—some had wasps, killer bees, and bats in them. He'd even told me he had a theory that the really big pythons used these old gold-mining shafts to brood their eggs in some of the shorter side shafts. "I think it's always best to look when you pass one of those shafts. A man wouldn't have much hope of coming out alive in a situation like that."

I looked up once and saw roots growing out of the ceiling of the shaft, trees from up above. I walked deeper into the dark. I looked back once, and the hole I'd entered had shrunken to the size of a silver dollar of light. What was I doing?

I inched forward until I saw the deep-black, sharply pointed scat piled at the end of the shaft. As the field guide explained, "Droppings are deposited at latrine sites," and this sure seemed to fit. Soon enough I was standing at the shaft's end. I'd somehow made it. I took a deep breath. I looked right, up the shaft toward where Ab had seen the genet. He had said that when he made the turn, he had to get down on his belly and crawl back to see it.

When I came back out, the heat hit me. It had been so much cooler in the shaft. Ab set up his camera and dribbled a can of tuna to maybe draw the genet into the frame. He and Chrissy, he said, would return the next week and retrieve the camera unless someone stole it, and maybe they'd have pictures of the cat.

Three

I stand neither in wilderness
nor fairyland
                              —Kathleen Jamie

The Bear in the Freezer

When we opened our college Environmental Studies Center in the piedmont of South Carolina, I was named director, and one of my first projects was to assemble a collection of tanned mammal pelts. I limited the collection to roadkills, mostly. This, I thought, would be an easy teaching moment for kids in our classes and outreach programs. We could show students what happened to animals if we were careless with our cars or if we decided they caused trouble for us. There was still a fairly abundant population of common mammals in upcountry South Carolina. By the time the bear arrived, we had pelts from roadkill otter, beaver, mink, red fox, gray fox, gray squirrel, and raccoon. A friend named Mike skinned them out for me. He explained he knew a Russian in the next county over who ran one of the largest remaining tanneries in the area, and this man would tan the hides for us at an educational discount. I saw our project as a way for some good (besides decomposition) to come of animal death.

Nobody in our environmental studies program enjoyed the death of wild animals. I was at the extreme end of the no-kill spectrum. I don't hunt. I remove bees and wasps from our screened porch with a plastic cup and live trap mice in the house. I relocate copperheads from terrified neighbors' yards and stop dozens of times a year to move box and snapping turtles from roadways. I saw the roadkill pelts project as a way to honor the dead and to come to terms personally with the carnage of wildlife killed on the local roads. I am also a social animal, so I saw the project as a chance to interact with Mike, who wasn't as squeamish about death as I was.

An unexpected source of skins came from our local wildlife officer, a man I had enjoyed talking with when he checked in with me from time to time. I told him of our educational project, and he liked the sound of it. He said that he would contribute any unusual new carcass that he came across, and at some point, "We might could get a roadkill bobcat, or even a bear from the northern part of the county."

Several weeks later, the officer called. "I got you a local bear," he said. "It's an adolescent and will fit in the freezer. Can you meet me down at the center?"

"How did it die?" I asked.

"It's a sad story," he said. "I'll tell you when I get there."

The dead bear looked pitiful wedged between the wheel well and the all-terrain vehicle in the back of the officer's pickup. He grabbed the bear's back legs and hauled it out on the lawn. "It's a small male," he said. "Maybe a yearling, seventy pounds or so."

I stared down at the bear's long, rangy legs and huge paws. The nails were jet black and curved slightly inward. The young bruin was skinny as a greyhound.

"How far from here was he?" I asked.

"Only about thirty miles, up in the northern county."

"Roadkill?"

"Naw, he got his head stuck inside a a big ol' mayonnaise jar. There's no way to tell how long his head was inside. Somebody reported him, and we finally tracked him down, but when I finally slid the jar off, he could barely stand. He was in terrible shape. I had no choice but to put him down."

It's not uncommon for all sorts of animals—cats, dogs, raccoons, bears—to get their heads caught in jars. The large discarded mayonnaise jar had functioned like one of those Chinese finger traps. Once the bear's head was inside, it wasn't coming out. As I looked at the animal, I imagined that the plastic jar was clear enough that he could see a hazy view of his surroundings. I tried to picture it but felt a little queasy, as if I had my own head inside that jar. I could see the bear stumbling blindly among trees and strangers, finally freed, only to die soon after. There was something beyond words about the bear with his head shrouded in plastic, slowly starving, and the world whirling around him like a bad hallucination.

Black bears in the South survived the twentieth century by retreating mostly to steep mountains, swamps, and canebrakes. They were hunted out in all other areas. More than a hundred years ago, in 1893, Theodore Roosevelt wrote a short piece called "The Black Bear" for *The Wilderness Hunter*, in which he explained how the black bear, before it was hunted out of most of its range, was second only to the deer in what he called "beasts of chase." Over most of its range, the wolf and the cougar quickly became scarce, but the black bear and whitetail deer stayed plentiful longer. According to Roosevelt, there were many reasons the bear was hunted with such relish. The meat was good, its fur could be valuable, and it offered the hunter excitement and even an occasional "slight spice of danger," though he also noted that black bears were really "not a very formable opponent."

In his account, Roosevelt described observing a black bear hunting in the open and how it turned over small logs and rocks, looking under each and every one, "shuffling along, rooting the ground...like a great pig."

In spite of being nearly hunted out, black bears have made a comeback in the Southeast. Their numbers are on the rise and there are regular legal hunts to cull the population at the coast and in the mountains. There are even signs they are pushing into the Piedmont, where our center is located. Every other year or so, a young bear is spotted along the creek behind the center, and I wonder how long it will be before a resident population makes it necessary for me to take down the bird feeders.

Since bears are a species in the midst of their improbable return to our area, I knew the pelt could be a good teaching tool, a way, at this stage of bear resurgence, to fully celebrate this bear's awful demise. As terrible as it sounds, the bear was like an organ donor. He'd unknowingly given his pelt and skull for science, or at least for show-and-tell natural history; he'd become a cadaver stored in our freezer, and several of his parts would survive him.

So we folded the bear up inside a garbage bag and hauled him to the freezer. As we closed the lid, the officer explained that after I'd skinned him out, he'd have to come back and harvest the gall bladder and the paws, since those could be sold on the black market, but that we were welcome to keep the skin and skull for educational purposes.

The next day, I told my colleagues about the dead bear so they wouldn't open the freezer and be surprised. It became a departmental joke with several of us: "The Bear in the Freezer."

A month passed after our dead bear was deposited, and I finally opened the Sub-Zero's top-loading lid, and it was not a joke anymore. The cold truth hit me in the face: I felt like I was looking down into a sarcophagus. The plastic bag had slipped off where one skinny leg had pushed out as it froze and stiffened. Rigor mortis waits for all creatures. His black bristly hair was sheathed with frost crystals like a tub of ice cream left too long in deep freeze.

With spring break approaching, I decided it was finally time to dispatch of the frozen bear. "You know that frozen-solid, seventy-pound adolescent bear in the center freezer?" I asked my colleagues. "How long do you think it will take to thaw it?"

"A twenty-pound turkey takes two days," one said. "Extrapolate from that."

"You definitely need to thaw him in the refrigerator," another added. "I wouldn't take a chance any other way."

"He won't fit in the refrigerator?," I said, "I think I have to thaw him at room temperature."

"Well, I hope your timing is good," the first colleague said. "That bear will smell pretty bad if he starts to rot."

I took my colleagues' advice and made sure the center's refrigerator was empty. Then I prepared the space for the bear's slow thaw. I removed the racks and opened up a space large enough for the frozen adolescent bear to fit. On the first Sunday of spring break, my friend Mike and I finally pulled the bear out. Mike grabbed a frozen solid leg, and I slipped both hands under the bear's skinny chin, holding on as if it were the handle of a jug. We both pulled upward, and he scraped past the frost on the deep freezer's sides. When we had him free, Mike balanced the bear's folded carcass on the freezer's lip, and I worked a second, thick contractor's garbage bag over him, just in case he leaked as he thawed. Then I opened the refrigerator, we tucked the bagged bear in, and closed the door. We would check back in a week and see if the bear had thawed enough to skin it out.

A week later, Mike met me at the center to finish our project and remove the pelt and skull for our collection. We opened the door to the center, and what hit us in the face was the unforgettable smell of rotten bear. The air was oily with the putrid stink of decayed flesh. I went straight to the lab and saw the thawed bear on the floor. Apparently, somewhere mid-thaw, he had slumped forward, pushed open the refrigerator, and toppled out. I was horrified but Mike began to laugh. "Guess you shoulda duct-taped that door shut."

We dragged the smelly, bagged bear to the back deck, then down the steps to the yard. When we pulled off the bags, Mike rolled him over on his back and rubbed his hand hard across the bear's belly. A hank of black hair came loose. "That's always the first place the hair slips," Mike explained. There would be no bear pelt in our collection. The Russian would have to wait for another road-kill.

"Let's just cut off the head," I said to Mike. "At least we can salvage the skull."

Mike pulled out his Buck knife, kneeled before the

dead carcass, and went to work. He rolled the bear from back to belly and held the head up and cut across the bottom of the neck at the base of the skull. Then he cut the backside. He'd done this procedure many times with deer heads. When he turned the head ninety degrees from the body, I heard the vertebrate popping, and the head twisted off.

After Mike removed the head, I called the wildlife officer and told him what had happened. He said he was sorry and to just dispose of the bear as we saw fit. We hauled the headless carcass to a remote patch of woods and laid it out for the vultures and coyotes to recycle.

And the skull? I froze the severed head and a week later took it over to our maintenance shop, where a friend rigged a wire cage to hold it, stood back and fired a high-pressure cleaning hose at the target until black hair and hunks of white flesh flew off in all directions. Then I hauled the cage, with the raw skull in it, back to the center and tied it to a tree in the woods where no one would see or smell it. I went back in six weeks and the skull was still inside the cage, clean and intact.

The incident with the dead bear took place more than a decade ago. When I retired, I brought the bear skull home and put it in my study, like an ancient *memento mori* ("Remember you must die") to sit on top of the case where I store my field journals. Other reminders of mortality would be less gruesome—a clock, an extinguished candle, rotting fruit, flowers past their bloom. But the idea of a black bear skull once trapped inside a jar was too compelling to leave behind. I look up and remember that, like the bear, I too will die, reminded by the skull, with its white two-inch canines and ghostly eye sockets.

An adult black bear in the wild can live almost twenty years. They are smart survivors—and if they can avoid hunters, roads, and charges of turning into a "bad bear" nuisance incapable of reform, there is little to threaten them in their long lives. That young, curious black bear might still be alive had he not stared death in its greasy face. I plan to keep the skull until I die, and then I plan to have it returned to the center. When I sit to write, the bear says to me, "Get down first and smell the earth. Get close to it... How deep the soul can delve. How dark the passage."

Newt Love

When I was twenty-three, in 1978, I left the South and moved to Port Townsend, Washington, to pursue my love of poetry. I grew homesick quickly, not for grits, humidity, and the Blue Ridge Mountains, but for the reptilian and amphibian tumult of the subtropics.

The Olympic National Park near Port Townsend had but fifteen amphibian and two snake species, the rubber boa and the garter snake. My love felt stunted. I looked into ditch-sides and onto sunny rubble and felt an absence. In my native South Carolina piedmont, there are thirty-seven amphibian species (twenty salamanders and seventeen frogs) and forty-five reptile species (nine turtles, nine lizards, and twenty-seven snakes). I ached for that absence.

My friend Richard Kerridge grew up a quarter of a world away, with far fewer species. Richard's debut memoir/natural history/conservation manifesto *Cold Blood* is about catching and caring for reptiles and amphibians in England. In it, I learned the story of a boy's enduring love for the charismatic cold-blooded fauna of the British Isles, and we are told, in no uncertain terms, why (and how) such admiration for these underserved orders is so important: "Something attracts us when we are young, and enters our imagination, becoming the doorway to adventure. Reptiles and amphibians gave me sensations of discovery, sensations of hunting, sensations of the world as infinite, leading us on."

In the first few pages of the first chapter, the present-time narrator lays out the origins of his life-long pattern of love for reptiles and amphibians and shows us its worth through memory, anecdote, and studied reflection. He also tells us how this love twines deeply around human relationships with friends (a compelling kid named "Micro" and a troupe of bike riders and toad catchers) and family, particularly his father, a man wounded in the Second World War and whom the narrator describes as a "snob and a bully."

But this is no tell-all memoir. The father in the story is no mere foil to adolescent rebellion. Throughout the story, the hurt Richard felt as a boy is seen through the lens of the adult narrator as necessary and even therapeutic. As Richard says of these childhood obsessions near the end of his narrative: "If something was your passion in childhood, if it became your symbolic language and ground of your battles, then that is a reason to return to it throughout your life."

And this "world as infinite" emerges forthwith. In prose often breaking into lyricism and rapture, Richard writes of his first sighting of a native amphibian: "It started with a golden newt in a black bog. I was ten." Here, at the book's beginning, Richard enters a lyrical mode describing this first encounter, and the language turns into a rollicking cascade of description and delight: pools glitter, surrounded by "clumps of ribbony pale brown grass, rising out of black slime" where "an oily film gleamed on the surface." How could one not think of Dylan Thomas and "Fern Hill" here?

This poetic quality continues throughout, but what's most impressive about this narrative is the way Richard is able to tie up the strands of this braid of prose. In one section, he's recounting the long-ago tales of critter-catching in the ditches and dunes, and in another, he's sketching out the natural history of toads and newts, and then in another, he's assessing his adolescent relationship with his family. Richard has a knack for knowing when to shift voices and when to linger on a personal detail, such as the construction of his private reptile and amphibian "museums" and when we readers need to have background.

One of the most interesting (and important) qualities Richard brings to this work is his ability to place us in an imagined point of view of the animals themselves. He does this once he has convinced us entirely that he understands the associated cultural issues: "Simply to renounce anthropomorphism—to attempt to stop doing it—would be to separate the natural world from the world of human meaning. It would be a refusal to recognize the wild world as part of our home, where we find emotional sustenance." He says the trick is "not to seek to expel [anthropomorphism] but instead, when we use it, to give precise attention" and to keep contact "with our perception of the otherness of wild creatures."

With that in mind, Richard draws us flawlessly into the imagined world of common toads squished on a busy motorway: "Tires have skidded on them...pale flesh on the black road." But then he conjures their toad feelings: "What sense of danger do toads feel, as the wheels approach?... What hits them might as well be an asteroid. Is the pond-music strong in their heads to the very last second? There is consciousness. Then it is gone."

Reading Richard's book is like picking up one of those pieces of tin warming in the spring sun and finding underneath, in my own imagination, his slumbering slow worm or smooth snake or common toad. The book offers such surprises. Richard's prose warms me like that spring sun. I hunt on after reading, chasing our own childhood passions and remembering my own lost disappointments and joys of discovery.

Throwing Stars

—after Loren Eiseley

When I was a child growing up in the 1960s, a vacation was something I never took for granted, but when we had them in the summer, they always oscillated between a mountain cabin on a rocky river at Chimney Rock Park and a trip to the South Carolina beach. Up at Chimney Rock, I'd roam the boulder-strewn Rocky Broad's edge looking for water snakes I thought I could kill with a braided-leather tourist bullwhip from the knickknack shop at park's main gate. I never killed a snake, but the hunts sharpened my outdoor skills and observations.

The beach meant a week at a motor court on the Isle of Palms. It was a long drive from Spartanburg to the ocean. I'd go down with my mother and her boyfriend. My days were spent swimming or crabbing with a chicken neck near the stone jetty at Breech Inlet, then selling my catch for a quarter a piece on the highway above.

There wasn't a lot of difference between beach vacations in South Carolina, no matter who you were. Everybody wanted the same things—access to the ocean, a sea breeze in a time before widespread air conditioning, and local fried seafood, sometimes even caught on the end of a string.

Now it's January, and I'm at Hilton Head Island, where my wife Betsy's gone on vacation her entire life. It isn't high season, so the beach is almost deserted. It's low tide, with bright sun and warm air. There are only a few people strolling between the remnant dunes and winter ocean, and we can even let the dog off the leash. In high season, Murphy would only be welcome early morning and late evening on Hilton Head beaches, the heat of the day reserved for human sun worshippers.

On Murphy's first run along the shore, I see starfish by the hundreds washed up, and I conjure a literary relationship with place. I think of Loren Eiseley's essay "The Star Thrower," about a lonely man the writer encounters throwing starfish back into the sea, a "perfect circle of compassion from life to death and back to life again."

I reach down and toss a starfish back. I look out to sea and think about eternity as I know Loren Eiseley would expect me to do.

Then our short-legged beagle changes course and pulls me away from my literary musing. He runs high up on the beach, slinging the loose sand behind him. As he sniffs his way south, I stop and cast my gaze from the starfish on the shore to the beachfront houses. I focus on two in particular, one a low, one-story model with a screened porch all the way across the front, one of the original oceanside Sea Pines houses; and the other a brand-new, three-story stucco palace, what many would call a McMansion, with open balconies and faux classic column flourishes. "That mansion's the result of a teardown," Betsy explains, coming up behind me. "It looks like the new generation doesn't like screened porches."

Until I started coming down to Hilton Head with my new family, my relationship with the place was entirely literary. I'd read about what developer Charles Fraser created on Hilton Head in the 1950s and 1960s, but I knew Fraser mostly through John McPhee's classic 1980s portrait of him in *Encounters with the Archdruid*, when he was trying to develop Cumberland Island. In that book Fraser acts as a foil for the Sierra Club's David Brower, "the archdruid." Back then, Fraser told McPhee that he regarded all conservationists as druids (religious figures who sacrifice people and worship trees), but I think he'd be glad to see Eiseley's "star thrower" practicing his ancient art on the Sea Pines beach.

Fraser's been dead now for some time. He lost control of Sea Pines Plantation (now known as Sea Pines Resort) in the 1980s, and it's since changed hands several times. Fraser is now considered a planning visionary, a golden-age grandparent of the sustainability/new urbanism movement, even the inventor of the modern resort style, but Sea Pines Plantation has followed other models through the years after a bankruptcy or two. Fraser's original vision of the vast forest preserve, a thousand-acre green space in the middle of the development, has been compromised, and many of his original design standards have been relaxed.

I'm drawn to Charles Fraser's original Sea Pines vision, but I think he would have been skeptical of what's happened to his creation. This vision of Sea Pines architecture—the screened porches we so love, large Asian overhangs, roofs with little slope, earth-tone colors, and native plants rather than formal Southern boxwoods—is getting harder to find along the bike trails. Everybody carries around in their heads clichéd phrases that help form their worldview. Two chestnuts I often trot out are William Faulkner's "The past is never dead. It's not even past," and another I often attribute to the Shakers, "Every force evolves a form." Both echo in my brain as I look up into the dunes at Sea Pines, and each makes my heart ache in a different way. The motor court where we stayed at the Isle of Palms was flattened in Hurricane Hugo, and the old Sea Pines from the mid-sixties is a disappearing past. Someday, I imagine the last of these original small Sea Pines ocean homes will be torn down and replaced.

When I look up beyond the dune, I see simple human desire on display, and I realize how uncomfortable I can get with modernity and change, especially at the beach. When I look the other way, out at the ocean, I get a hint of what I'm looking for: time and the tides, for to look at the ocean is to touch the eternal cycles. Murphy wanders back down to the tide line, and I follow and toss another star. Maybe that's the whole point of vacation, to bring up such stark contrasts. Maybe that's all that really matters.

Concerning Turtles

I stop and move turtles when I see them crossing the road. I've done this all my life, well, at least since I began driving, and I've done it all over the country. You may do it too. Sometimes it's easy, as in the case of box turtles, who sometimes close up in their shells when I approach and pick them up; or musk turtles or mud turtles, who tend to sit passively or run in midair like cartoon characters as I lift them; or the rare soft-shelled turtle I rescued once, who stared up at me, past its needle nose, uncertain what had happened. Other times, it's more difficult, as with snapping turtles, who are usually large and aggressive and not interested in my help, thank you.

In the South, they say if a snapping turtle bites, it won't let go until it thunders. I don't want to prove or disprove this folk wisdom, so when I move a snapping turtle, I am very careful, but I do it anyway. Why do I do it? Why do I move turtles off the road—always in the direction they are heading? Why stop my speeding pickup, pull over, get out, and run, sometimes, to get to the turtle before the next car or truck? In my case, this turtle rescue is very complex. First, I can't stand seeing turtles crushed on the highway. I am cursed with a certain kind of animal awareness, and I don't know why or how it happened exactly. I always notice crushed turtles, as I notice all "roadkill." But I also usually notice living wild animals on the side of the roads as well: deer pondering whether to cross and when; hawks on wires hunting the verges; vultures on the shoulder, feasting on what didn't make it; snakes on the center line, basking on the warm pavement. I see them all. And I can't pass their presences by. That's what I mean by cursed. I can't get past animal presences, and the presence that is most disturbing to me is their dead presence, and I want to do all I can to prevent those deaths—so I even slow down for suicide squirrels as well as help turtles across the road. By "can't get past their dead presence," I don't exactly mean that I believe in ghosts, though there is that hint in what I say, that even in death animals are still here if you see them die, or see the aftermath of their deaths. They are ghosted into my mind by their presence, and I can't forget them, and I suggest that it's because they have such long residence in places, and their residence stretches back and forward, at least until their populations are eradicated from areas. This is happening at an alarming rate with box turtles in particular, a species now listed as "vulnerable" with "decreasing population" as their conservation status.

Animal presence is also about time, or more precisely, duration. We humans are literally passing through compared to how long box turtles have lived in their particular landscapes. Even the roads that are their undoing are recent, though many roads were first trails, and before that, animal traces, especially big roads like interstates, which follow routes across landscapes that may go back tens of thousands of years. Did you know some believe that human beings should be listed as an endangered species because we meet all the listing requirements?

But I move turtles for another more complex reason too, one that's maybe really "out there." I believe that over a lifetime (mine), if I move enough turtles across enough

roads I might actually make a biological difference to tur-
tle-population dynamics. I might increase the chances that
in the spring, when a male turtle starts to roam its small
territory in search of a female, or a gravid female turtle
searches to find some sand or dirt to dig a nest hole, it will
find it and pass on its genes and assure that there will be
more turtles. What prompted me to think this way? I don't
know. Why would I possibly care? Maybe it's karma.
There's a guy named John Scott Foster who believes, and
shall we say preaches, that moving turtles off roads is good
karma. And who is to say he's wrong? In the humanities,
the recent field of animal studies examines questions and
issues that arise from more traditional humanistic and scientific ideas about animals. I like to think that what I'm
participating in when I move turtles from the road is the
fieldwork side of animal studies. I like to think that I am
questioning some traditional ideas about animals through
my actions. Animal studies seems to confirm:

—Animals are not dumb.
—Animals are not machines with no souls.
—Animals are not essentially different than humans.
—We do not deserve dominion over animals.

Animal studies takes animals seriously as subjects of
thought and activity. How is it possible to take turtles seriously? How is our humanity defined in relation to animals? How do representations of animals create under-
standings (and misunderstandings) of other species?
Animal studies pays close attention to the ways that humans anthropomorphize animals, and animal studies asks

how humans might avoid bias in observing other creatures. Animal studies strives to reexamine traditional ethical, political, and epistemological categories in the context of a renewed attention to and respect for animal life. In this way, it verges on ethics. Is it simply wrong to run over animals in the road? Why would our life be shattered if we ran over a child, but it could be business as usual if we hit a deer or a turtle?

There is also an assumption that focusing on animals might clarify our human knowledge. As Claude Lévi-Strauss famously said, animals are "good to think." What does that mean? Let's consider for a moment the presence of turtles in our lives.

Worldwide, there are more than three hundred species of turtles, ranging from six-foot leatherback sea turtles weighing two thousand pounds to three-inch, five-ounce padloper tortoises. In other words, there is huge diversity when we talk about turtles. Evolutionary history shows us they have been around for two hundred million years. And we have various attitudes toward them. Many people still eat them. Many people trap snapping turtles in ponds because they eat fish and baby ducks. Lots of people keep turtles for pets. Asians in particular import millions of wild turtles illegally. Spotted turtles can go on the black market in Asia for $2,000 each. Diamondback terrapins from the eastern North America coastal marshes, $3,000. The trade in illegally caught US turtles to Asia is said to be worth tens of millions. And yet six US states allow unlimited turtle trapping. Even still, here in Spartanburg County we are surrounded by turtles. There is probably a wild box turtle or two living within a half mile of you as you read this.

Are turtles dumb? Well, traditionally turtles have been considered quite limited in their intelligence, but in tests, some reptiles, particularly some turtles, do respectably well. The wood turtle is widely believed to be one of the most intelligent turtles. They are considered to have high levels of curiosity and show abilities to solve mazes. In the wild, they have been shown to "trick" earthworms by stomping their front feet to bring them to the surface. They are the only turtles known to do this. Are turtles machines with no souls? We used to think so. The philosopher Descartes thought so. He believed animals were incapable of thought. This, to him, implied a fundamental difference between us and all other animals. Not so much anymore. How are turtles different from humans? This is a very good question, and I almost want to reverse it—how are we similar?

Do we deserve dominion over turtles? Whether we deserve it or not, we claim it. I think I'll leave this one unanswered. One reason I care about turtles is I want to know about them. You see, when I learned a few things about box turtles, I started caring more. What did I learn that was interesting? I learned they live out their lives in small territories, some as small as 750 feet on a side. I learned that they are so connected to their particular place that to relocate them is practically a death sentence. They have a homing instinct. If they are relocated, they have to work a great deal harder to make a living too. Like us, they are omnivores. They eat slugs, worms, insects, salamanders, fish, birds, frogs, eggs, fungi, berries, and roots.

Male box turtles have red eyes, are larger, and the males have concave plastrons; the females have yellow-

and-brown eyes and flat plastrons. The average life span of adult box turtles is fifty years, while a significant portion live more than one hundred years. That is, unless they get run over by a car. I'm trying and sort through some ideas I usually wouldn't think of. I hope animal presence is one of those ideas.

Rare Birds

I

On the roundabout when you leave the Marsh Harbour airport, the first thing tourists see is a giant, colorful, concrete Abaco parrot in the mowed-center circle. The Abaco National Park on the south end of Great Abaco in the Bahamas is twenty thousand acres of pine flats and a slender scrubby zone of salt-tolerant hardwoods along the ocean. The park protects, among other indigenous birds and wildlife, the foraging and nesting range of eight thousand endangered Abaco parrots. These parrots are unique among their New World kin as they nest in limestone sinkholes among the pines.

This was my fifth trip to the six-mile-long island of Elbow Cay in the northern Bahamas, a twenty-minute ferry ride across the water from where the planes land in Marsh Harbour. The first two times I was here was in the mid-80s accompanying January short-term college classes. On those trips, taught by a good friend, I was a guest, a sort of writer-in-residence, and my thoughts were often public, focused both inward (because of the class) and outward toward the exotic surrounding sea. I had never spent time snorkeling on coral reefs or watching the ocean every day from a porch facing the wild Atlantic, so my class observations often focused on how we might get more in touch with the place. On Elbow Cay was the first time I ever really understood what Rachel Carson, someone familiar with coastlines, really meant when she titled her 1951 book, her first, *The Sea Around Us.*

Twelve years later, in 2000, after Betsy and I married, we came back for a week with three of her friends, renting a boat out of Marsh Harbour and sailing to Elbow Cay, Man of War Cay, and Great Guana Cay. On that trip, I explored the coral reefs even more intimately, my attention focused on what still seemed off-shore wilderness, a landscape below the surface, vast and protected from the horror of on-shore inland development and industrial tourism that had, by that time, become a cliché in the Bahamas.

On my fourth return, in 2010, Betsy and I rented a house for a week in Hope Town on the settlement's historic main drag between the lower and main ferry dock, and we explored the north end of the island as our two boys went out daily to be certified as sailboat captains by a local outfit.

I've kept journals and poems from every trip to Elbow Cay, and I remember what they contain—the expected sense of wonder for a writer, the discovery of a new world, an alien landscape. I am a man who grew up far from easy access to such watery realms, and for me, they have always contained the sense of otherness and strangeness, that flush of natural riches. "Keats Never Snorkeled" I embroidered onto a white cap after visiting the Abacos the first time in the 1980s, and I wore that cap for years, perplexing my friends. This statement, for me, summed up my sense of artistic privilege in the late twentieth century.

Now, twenty-two years into the next century, it's different. In the ten years since we had last been on Elbow Cay, I'd become aware of many other layers to my own privilege and how much I had taken for granted on my first trips there. I had come to own some of the ways that the very life I lead degrades and diminishes the island where I vacation, where I had experienced my poetic reveries. Add to all that a shift in my teaching life from English to environmental studies, and the result was a basic deepening of my perspective. Because of climate change, it was also now downright impossible to visit this low carbuncle of limestone, sand, and coral without thinking about the coming challenges of sea level rise to all affected, land, sea, and air creatures, including the long-term human settlers of the island, both Black and White.

So, when I returned the fifth time, I did some preliminary research on how the native conch reserves in the Bahamas have been depleted 80 percent since I visited in the late 1980s. The conch fishing had collapsed in Bermuda and in the Florida Keys in the 1970s. It's looking likely now that the same might happen in the Bahamas. The culinary symbol of the cays—that first order of conch fritters—went down a little uneasily once I was conscious of the pressures on the fishery.

I looked up the parrots, too. Once they could be found on Abaco, New Providence, San Salvador, Long Island, Crooked Island, Acklins, and Great Inagua, but now they are isolated and found only on Abaco and Great Inagua. Columbus had reported them in 1492 when he landed in the New World, so they have quite a distinction of being one of the first species reported in the explorer's journals, making them sort of like those Americans who look for their names on the roll of the Mayflower. Many think that the Abaco and Great Inagua parrots are a distinct population, though they are still not deemed a separate species. They have been protected since 1952, and unlike the conch, their conservation story has an upside: the parrot population is now considered stable, with maybe more than five thousand birds on Abaco and perhaps as many as twelve thousand on Great Inagua. Now the threat to their numbers comes mostly from encroaching development, feral cats, land crabs, and the pet trade.

Sometimes I long for the innocence of those first trips to the islands, when I was in my thirties and believed that when I visited places like Elbow Cay, I was witness to a play that would never close. I know there is no rolling back time, no recovering the innocence of travels enjoyed in my youth, no "easy in the islands," no more living in a Jimmy Buffett song. Now every issue is only a click away from ecological studies and current research into the ways the world has been compromised in the water-weary Anthropocene. And, as if to complicate things even more, the morning we went over to look for the parrots, off the ferry trudged all the early island workers, Black Bahamians from Marsh Harbour, twenty minutes and eleven dollars across the Sea of Abaco each way, the day laborers on construction sites, the restaurant workers, the custodians in the tourist lodges. No one looked up as we passed. No one greeted us with the usual lilting "hello" you get on the streets of Elbow Cay as we traipsed off on our adventure in search of a feel-good sighting of the rare Abaco parrots.

But I never considered not going to look for the parrots. What would that prove? I was there, and so were the parrots. The parrots didn't need me, but a forty-year bioblitz confirmed that I needed them. We were in the islands, easy or not, so why not take a morning and go back over the water to Abaco to commune with the island's rarest wildlife?

II

We met our naturalist guide, Reg Paterson, at the Marsh Harbour ferry landing. Reg, too, was descended from original white British settlers of the Abacos, so Reg's Loyalist pedigree is European rather than African, unlike the workers we'd seen depart in Hope Town. His day job was that of surveyor, but his passion was showing those interested the natural history of Abaco, like Betsy and me, around. Reg was a slender man with glasses, a neat moustache. He was dressed in khakis, soft brown boots, and a light-blue plaid shirt, maybe so he could pass for either surveyor or nature guide, depending on the appointment. He'd come prepared with an Igloo of chilled water, his binoculars, and a map falling apart from being folded and unfolded. I asked him what the locals think of the parrots. "Generally, Bahamians, Black or White, are mostly indifferent to conservation," he explained. "It's baby steps—grouper fishing now has one closed season a year. They're beginning to understand they have to protect the resources."

As we exited the harbor area, Reg filled us in on his life. He'd lived in the Abacos fifty years, coming to Elbow Cay when he was thirteen with his family, which had roots there in the 1780s. His father had been in real estate and was also an amateur botanist and naturalist who'd written a book about native flora of the Bahamas. As a child, Reg had accompanied him on field trips. Now his double Trip

Advisor stickers in the pickup's back window announced his tilt back toward his father's avocation.

Driving out of Marsh Harbour, on the only road south, the parking lot and low-rise sprawl of a tourist town quickly turned to the native pines, mostly thin pencils with flourishes of needles at their crown and bases scorched by a recent wildfire. As we passed into this more rural country, Reg outlined the land-use history of Great Abaco. After World War II, mechanical clearance with bulldozers made industrial-scale agriculture possible in the limestone and pine flats. Sugarcane farmers made a go of it, but the crop was only minimally prosperous and ultimately unsustainable. Now, all those fields had returned to the pine trees we saw as we drove toward the island's south end.

Reg had guided many ecotourists like us, so he knew what we really wanted to know—how likely was it we'd see parrots? "The park's so huge—you can often hear the birds squawking," he said. "But they're often in the distance and you can't see them."

III

In order to hedge his bets, Reg had an almost guaranteed parrot encounter in an unsuccessfully developed subdivision just north of the national park. We'd go there first, he explained, drive the almost deserted roads, roll down the windows, and just listen. I was used to this rolling form of nature survey, so I wasn't surprised. I looked forward to seeing the island at whatever pace Reg provided.

As we covered the dozen or so miles south, the sun climbed quickly in the subtropic skies, and the air itself seemed naked. It was dry and hot by the time we reached the breezy-sounding development called Bahama Palms Shores. As we entered, Reg rolled his window down and I did the same. We were listening, mostly for parrots, the air conditioning blasting to keep Betsy cool in the truck's jump seat.

We cruised slowly past a few neat houses tucked back into the thick coastal scrub, including one called "Parrot Perch." For every neat house, though, there were dozens of undeveloped lots, some not at neat as others. We passed a double-wide trailer with a wormy cat out front. Then one of the lots had a small yellow house on it with seven cats just hanging around. Reg explained a woman everybody called "the cat lady" had lived there, and quickly segued into how feral cats, like these, had always been one of the primary challenges in stabilizing the parrot population further south in the park. Reg said that park wardens monitored the nesting sites and humanely removed cats when they became a problem. I watched these potential parrot poachers licking their paws and lolling around under the coco plums and thought about the worldwide problem of cats and wild birds. And here it was again. I hoped they could be controlled.

In spite of the cats, parrots seemed to like it here in the subdivision, Reg suggested. There was plenty of food—fruit and seeds—and he saw a small group of birds so regularly that this was his go-to spot for bird groups.

"Why are the parrots here and not in the park?" I asked.

Maybe they were bachelors, Reg speculated, or immature birds wandering north of the nesting ground in the national park.

"Did you hear that squawking?" Reg asked, as we turned back onto the main road into the subdivision and stopped the truck. We threw open the doors and we all three piled out. "Over there," Betsy said, spotting the silhouettes of two parrots in a bare Australian pine tree between us and ocean. We drove closer, piled out once again, and it was indeed the rare Abaco parrot, hanging out in a pine, green coats flashing against the blue sky and the coral ascot under their chins flaring like skyrockets!

We crept slowly forward on a sand drive on one of the few developed lots but were stopped by a gate. In spite of it, we were able to get close enough to watch one grooming itself. The two parrots didn't seem concerned we were there. One bird kept grooming, but the other left the pine and flew lower to a banana palm. It squawked, sounding like a creaking door. Then the grooming bird flew into a gumbo-limbo and sat for a long time, as if posing for Betsy's clicking camera. After we'd watched for ten minutes, they both disappeared deeper into the brush. Reg pointed out how camouflaged they became when not squawking and how you could lose them amid all the green.

"What's the most you've ever seen?" I asked him.

"Once, years ago," Reg said, "I was hunting in the south near a water hole, and a big flock of parrots came in for their evening drink. They were putting up quite a squawk, about fifty of them. It was almost intimidating. I gave up the hunt. With that noise I knew nothing would come in. I packed up and went home."

IV

After the brief parrot communion, Reg drove us one street over to a friend's private garden. At first, I didn't realize it was a garden, though once we were inside it took on a magical closed-in feel, with dozens of blooming trees, some, like a giant fruiting papaya, with green bowling balls clustered near the top.

The friends maintained a small feeder, and right away Reg pointed out a greater Antillean bullfinch, red on throat with a red eyebrow, that wasn't going to let our parrot tour deter its morning feeding. It hopped from limb to feeder perch, immune to us.

Walking around the garden, Reg picked up a good-sized hermit crab creeping through the yard. "Soldier crabs, we call them. Fifty years ago, my family would have eaten it. I don't really have any memories what they would have tasted like." I remembered from my reading that crabs sometimes ate parrot chicks, another worry besides the cats.

Then we walked to where the yard turned to a wall of brush. Reg pointed out a thick-billed vireo in a royal poinciana tree. "Its mate won't be far away. They are always calling out to each other to reassure they are close." The parrots chattering again, and we were hopeful they would land in the garden and we'd see them. We could hear them squawking as they retreated. Reg explained that vulture overhead had probably startled them, and "any large bird can be mistaken for a red-tailed hawk, one of their natural predators."

Once the parrots were gone, our eyes and attention

settled once again on the lower reaches of the garden. Reg pointed out a La Sagra's flycatcher and a bananaquit in quick succession, and then he began a remarkable botanical tour of our surroundings, and I thought how proud his father, the amateur botanist, would have been. Reg touched each plant as he passed it and gave us its common name, "rough-skinned lemon; mahoe, called cork tree; sour orange; sapodilla, which the Bahamians call 'dilleys'; scarlet plum; coco plum; red cedar, rare in the wild but still found in people's gardens; sweetwood, of which the bark is harvested and exported to Italy, used to flavor Campari; horseflesh, used for boat building; and cinnamon bark, which I use as bugs repellant when I can't get anything else."

V

It was only 9:15, and our three parrots would have to do for the moment. We had a few more hours to go. Doesn't it always happen this way? Whatever you anticipate happens unexpectedly or it doesn't happen at all. So much of interaction with the world is waiting, and then savoring, once it's happened, whatever that is.

We drove farther south and passed the Abaco National Park sign, and next to it, a derelict picnic table. We parked Reg's truck just off the main highway at a pullout for the Hole-in-the-Wall GSM site, where there is a tall transmission tower. Bahama swallows swirled in the heat, little black-and-white scissors doing laps around the tower. The real beauty and surprise were hundreds of Atala hairstreaks, tiny black-and-orange butterflies mobbing the dense underbrush.

I looked deep into the pines. As an inland soul, I craved deep deciduous forests, but here on Abaco was an expanse of forty-foot pines rooted on a dry sponge of crusty, porous limestone softened only by thickets of poisonwood.

Reg led us down a two-track logging road, a remnant from the latest harvest of the vast Abaco pine forest in the 1960s. Reg explained that loggers had left five seed pines per acre when they clear-cut but that he thought the trees probably needed thinning now, fifty years later. I heard the trilling of pine warbler, but mostly the woods were silent when we first entered them. Only as they swallowed us did they begin to enliven. To speed things along, Reg stopped, played his iBird Pro, and said, "A grassquit male is answering," and then something less clear answered in the distance and Reg put his glasses on it. "It's a warbler, I think. I glimpsed white wing bars."

Reg trained his glasses into the pines. It was a more subtle landscape than I expected and reminded me of young longleaf. I looked around. Through the canopy I watched a swinging raft of vultures. There was red-tail calling, and Reg said there was an old nest nearby; when the nest was active, they'd dive-bombed him as he walked below. I spotted a hummingbird sipping at a bright-red vine flower, and Reg soon confirmed, "Bahama woodstar." Then it flitted away right over the top of us. As we walked, Reg pointed out poisonwood we'd seen back in the subdivision. "Be careful. Black sap. That's when you know you have it, and by then it's too late."

Reg spotted the pine warbler we'd been hearing

sitting in a sapling pine, and then he pointed me toward a Bahama warbler in a pine working up and down the trunk like a nuthatch. And then we heard a mockingbird, and soon we got a good look at it, and it was a Bahama mocker! I'd really wanted to see the Bahama mockingbird, a little larger and a little darker than its northern cousins. Two of them were right before us, in residence in a pine, and they decided to really put on a concert of many unfamiliar songs.

A little farther along the two-track, Reg cued up his iBird Pro one more time, and a warbler song repeated over and over. Then, finally, he heard the bird he hoped would answer: "An olive-capped warbler!" Then he saw it in the nearby brush. Back at the truck, we poured some water out of the Igloo and watched a Cuban peewee sitting on a pine stub watching us, so close we could see the distinct white half-moon around its eye.

VI

Soon we drove a little further south and turned onto another gravel two-track road. Reg showed us on the map how the road continued eighteen miles to the remote Hole-in-the-Wall Lighthouse. He explained how he liked to drive a few miles on the road, but not all the way in, as the last several miles were terrible and best walked. The red-and-white lighthouse itself, out of commission, sits on a rocky coast, as far south as you can get on Abaco. Reg said it's hard to imagine the lives of the two families of keepers who lived there isolated for a hundred years.

We passed homemade national park signs nailed on

trees. One said "Plane Crash" and another "Parrot Ridge." Reg explained that the island's legacy in the 1990s as a drug-smuggling destination meant that Columbians would sometimes fly old planes and crash land in the pines, sometimes clearing a swath of trees to land them safely. Betsy was in the back seat, enjoying the stories, but maybe a little uncertain as to why we were headed into the bush with no apparent destination. I'd spent enough time with naturalists to know the ratio between seeing something and nothing is sometimes fairly high. Sometimes in college I would drive five hours with a friend on rural roads to catch one or two snakes thermoregulating on the pavement.

A mile or two through the forest, we finally stopped the truck on a high limestone ridge and stepped out to observe what Reg said was a dull-colored female western spindalis in the poisonwood. Soon after, a brightly colored male wandered through, the colors matching the bird on the cover of his bird guide. This spot worked as a nice culmination for our morningtide of pine-forest birds.

VII

Gilpin Point was our last stop on the way back to Marsh Harbour, a fully laid out subdivision on the Sea of Abaco. There was only one house there, where one guy lives, hermit-like, within the grid of rough, quiet limestone streets. Reg said the man was of Greek descent, and that his grandparents came to the Bahamas as sponge fishermen, that being another industry, along with shipping, sugarcane, and pineapples, that has come and gone from the

Abacos. The Greek lived quietly in a concrete house, set back in what Reg called "the corpus belt," the zone of scrub hardwoods yet uncleared where the parrots were known to feed. It was never clear whether the Greek owned all the undeveloped lots or whether he had taken on the role of caretaker, a sort of Robinson Crusoe on an island of failed real estate.

We stopped on the way to the beach to see a raft of white-cheeked pintail ducks on a briny mangrove pond. The Greek kept a container of corn on the dock to feed them. The ducks may have been my favorite birds of the outing, outshining even the brief appearance of the Abaco parrots at the other subdivision. Maybe it was their white cheeks and red nose patch, or their mottled cream bodies that tilted as they dabbed for sinking cracked corn. At the pond there was also a sunken boat, making everything seem even more ruinous. Between its swamped gunnels the water had turned a milky blue like glacial till.

We saw two black-necked stilts on the salt pond too, likely a nesting pair, as one was very agitated and even came out onto the sand road on impossibly long legs to click at us as we continued on to the beach.

The Greek kept up the beach access Gilligan's Island-style, with objects he'd collected—whatever colorful or odd that floated in—and maintained a very nice flush toilet. He'd arranged the junk into a sort of outsider art installation, with yellow netting hanging in the trees, tripods of driftwood with blue-and-white buoy balls hanging as pendulums, lounge tables made from discarded wire spools. Black storage boxes, pulled off the high tide line, held detritus sorted into categories—four-stroke engine oil bottles in one, scraps of black matting in another, one half full of clear milk bottles, a one-man cleanup operation. Reg said people came out on the weekends, as the Greek didn't seem to mind the company and sharing his deserted corner of Abaco with others.

It took an hour to get back to Marsh Harbor and another half hour to cross back to Elbow Cay again. Reg had his circuit down pat, five hours from door to door. Timing makes for a high rating on Trip Advisor and a fine morning in the pines. Reg knew how to introduce the world to the island's rare birds. Was I disappointed we didn't see parrots after the first brief but electric encounter in Bahama Palm Shores? Was I dispirited that the parrots nest in the limestone far from the park's two-tracks? I felt fine just knowing the parrots were out there, wary of cats and land crabs, safe from the stealthy poachers who would steal their young chicks for the pet trade. I don't have to lay eyes on everything in the world, I've concluded, and often what I see is more than enough.

Bird list for the day:
Abaco parrots (3), frigate bird, American kestrel, hairy woodpecker, Greater Antillean bullfinch, thick-billed vireo, black-whiskered vireo, Bahama swallows, bananaquit, black-faced grassquit, turkey vultures, Bahama woodstar, red-shouldered hawk, Bahama mockingbird, Cuban peewee, western spindalis, Bahama warbler, olive-capped warbler, white-cheeked pintail ducks, black-necked stilt.

Four

Two Elegies

Death steals everything except our stories.
—Jim Harrison

Wild God

The clock stopped, and I was closer than I had ever come to the world as it is made.

—James Kilgo, *Colors of Africa*

In 1999, only three years before cancer took James Kilgo, he thought that he was going to write an entire book about Ossabaw Island, an isolated sea island now owned by the state off the coast of Georgia. This project would have given Jim a chance "to seek the ghosts of the past amidst the wilderness of the present." Beginning in the late '90s, Jim made many visits to Ossabaw, including two with a small group of what we called back then "Southern nature writers." I was included on those trips, and I listened as Jim worked out in conversation his outline for a book about the island and struggled with ideas of a possible narrative structure for the book-length study. We all accepted that he had been chosen to write the island's story and watched and listened as he sorted through his materials. The two weekends on the island offered us an informal workshop on writing about Southern nature surrounded by the subject itself. All of us were teachers, and on those weekends, all students. We ate together, pondered the South and its complex environmental and deep social history, and on afternoon outings, explored Ossabaw's vast unpeopled interior and beaches. "What I want is for the island to get a grip on me," he wrote a little later.

Over the next several months, in a few phone calls,

Jim spoke of the trouble he was having shaping the story he wanted out of his contact with Ossabaw. At that time, I underestimated the seriousness of the block and thought my friend was merely struggling with the size and depth of the island's past. How could anyone possibly get the third-largest of the Georgia sea islands—a place with a human history dating back at least four thousand years, including four hundred years of European and African settlement—into a single book? By late 1999, Jim was facing an uncertain future in his battle with cancer, and he began seriously second-guessing his decision to write about Ossabaw. In June of that year, he had delivered a symposium talk entitled "The Earth Is the Lord's but He's Giving It to the Meek" in Sitka, Alaska, at the Island Institute. In Jim's remarks, he was honest about his cancer, saying in the second paragraph that his future was uncertain. He wondered aloud how, if Ossabaw was to be his last book, he could bear witness to his "faith in God the father, son, and Holy Ghost" in a narrative about the history and natural history of a barrier island. More poignant was Jim's question of the value of what one should be writing in the face of death.

When Jim's Sitka symposium talk turned up again it renewed my interest in these spiritual questions. In fall of 2012, upon opening to the table of contents of the special issue of *The Georgia Review*, I was confronted by two ghosts. First, the issue contained Jim's never-before-published talk, "The Earth Is the Lord's but He's Giving It to the Meek." I had already read the talk and handed it out to admirers of Jim's work, always marveling over the beauty of Jim's handwritten corrections in the margins of a photocopy Jim had given me. Like everything else about Jim—his conversation, his elegant sentences and images—his handwriting revealed his sensitivity and attention to grace notes.

As a writer and a mentor Jim remains with me, and the reappearance of the Sitka talk made him appear a little like Hamlet's ghost intoning "Remember me" from the castle's parapets. After all, it was the year I turned sixty-one that it reappeared, Jim's age when he died. What better prompt to take stock of a question Jim asked in his Sitka talk: "Why write anyway?"

The Sitka talk is a glimpse into the mind and faith of a Christian nature writer. Jim saw himself as a writer with "strong affinities for both God and nature," and as a Southerner, he had "grown up down there going hunting and fishing on Saturday, and attending church on Sunday—at least, through my generation we did." Because of this, Jim saw himself as part of a spiritual tradition of writing about the natural world that included Annie Dillard, Barry Lopez, and Terry Tempest Williams, three writers Jim admired deeply and referred to often. The talk in Sitka gave Jim an "opportunity to hack out a place to stand, to articulate an environmental ethic rooted in the center that holds for me," and he took his stand.

In his brief talk, Jim showed how he was opposed to the synthesis of most "eco-theology," which might include a blend of Emerson, New Age, and animism. He quoted the late Father Thomas Berry, an eco-theologian and Roman Catholic priest, and former California senator Tom Hayden as examples of proponents of the sort of pop-eco-theology. Jim could not accept a synthesis of all religions, including paganism, because it "leaves out the person and purpose of Jesus Christ." Jim was not judgmental though. In spite of his strong personal faith, he accepted the differences between us.

Jim used his own experience at this important environmental symposium to show how a deep and vital Christian commitment could be squared with contemporary environmentalism. He used the Sitka talk to show his love of the natural world and how it had animated his work for so long. It was his way, finally, of saying that he could not love the earth without also professing his love of Jesus Christ. In the end, he settled on two key points for the Christian environmentalists to consider: they must practice stewardship, and they must love other people in spite of the likely presence of sin, for everything wasn't sunshine and light. "Sin is sin," he said near the end of the talk, whether it involved "abusing children or poisoning the salt marsh with toxic waste."

Considering Jim's eventual death in 2002, I can now see in retrospect why, as a believing Christian, he may have questioned the power of Southern nature and the set of experiences that Ossabaw offered—speculation on deep native wildness, animism, and the possible ritualisms that shaped it—and instead left himself open for the invitation to experience another landscape through a safari that would become his final book-length spiritual memoir, *Colors of Africa*. There, first alluded to in the Sitka talk, Jim returned to two of his earliest passions, his Christian God and the culture of hunting.

I have called myself an agnostic most of my post-college life. I was born into the Methodist Church, much like

Jim, but I never joined as an adult. I did join a nondenom-inational youth group called Young Life my senior year in high school. In college I worked for Young Life the spring of my freshman year. I was what I guess now would be called an evangelical. I met often with the campus Young Life group, read the Bible, sang, prayed, and began taking college religion classes with vague thoughts of going to di-vinity school or seminary. I cobbled together a scattershot of random religion and English classes into an interdisci-plinary degree and graduated.

Becoming a poet was my vocational direction, so in-stead of divinity school, I ended up with two abandoned attempts at grad school in English: once at Middlebury's Bread Loaf School of English the summer after college, and once more, a year later, at the University of Virginia as a Hoyns Fellow in poetry, followed by a year in their brand-new MFA program.

After that, a period emerged in the late 1980s/early 1990s when the deeply spiritual side of me surfaced. For more than a decade, I was part of a community at the Nantahala Outdoor Center where I practiced Buddhist meditation and read in popular Buddhist literature and had audiences with visiting Zen teachers at the center. In that way, I fit the profile of a pretty typical New Ager, something I probably held onto longer than any other in-tellectual system (if you can call it that) besides environ-mentalism. In the late '80s, I even got caught up in Robert Bly's Men's Movement, which I like to call "The Myth Movement" to hint at what I saw as the depth of its story-telling. I attended a handful of weekend retreats with the gurus of the movement—Robert Bly, Michael Meade, and

James Hillman, including the weekend Bly's *Iron John* came out. I taught "Hero's Journey" freshman courses in my early years at Wofford, introducing a generation of young students to Bly, Carl Jung, and Joseph Campbell.

This was also the period when I was practicing a sort of New Age pilgrim paganism as well—with regular visits to Native American sacred sites such as the Kituhwa Mound in North Carolina, the Serpent Mound in Ohio, and Wyoming's Big Horn Medicine Wheel. I was inspired at the time to haul in rocks and build my own medicine wheels, culminating in the one I added to my backyard in Spartanburg the year of my first teaching job at Wofford College in '88. I had a notion that any place could be sacralized, believing, as Black Elk said, that a sacred center could be anywhere and everywhere, even a backyard in up-country South Carolina. By building a medicine wheel and walking it in a ritual way every day, I imagined getting in touch with some sort of deeper earth energies. This also played itself out in the circumambulation/settlement actions that I documented in my book *Circling Home*, about building our house in the suburbs of Spartanburg, and in my essay "Circumambulation," about walking the Gary Snyder/Philip Whalen Buddhist pilgrimage route on Mount Tamalpais near San Francisco with one of my students. It was through these experiments that I explored how a particular faith might determine one's relationship to place in a deep manner.

Calling myself an agnostic, I anxiously looked and listened for spiritual connection everywhere, like a spiritual metal detector, seeking the ping; for me, the "truer" sound was the deepest ping. In my deeply Methodist-Buddhistinflected agnosticism, I thought of spirituality as a universal bedrock that creation sits upon, like the *Star Wars* "force." Religions were human constructions layered on top of this metaphoric bedrock, like sediment, with the oldest layer being the various paganisms followed by the big world religions—Hinduism, Buddhism, Christianity, Islam—laid down as the religious floods receded century by century, the latest layer being the muddy effluvium of worldwide secularism.

Agnostics can be considered among the "religiously unaffiliated," those who say they believe in "nothing in particular" about God. This idea of believing in nothing in particular does not appeal to me, so now I even question my agnosticism. I believe in everything in particular, the ten thousand things, the great bursting forth of life into myriad forms, worlds without end. I fit squarely in the camp that believes that the existence of the ultimate cause (like a God) and the essential nature of things are unknown and always unknowable, a quality I call "mystery." I've spent much of my life worshipping at mystery's altar. I balk at the agnostic idea that human knowledge is limited to only experience, so I guess I'd have to say that I'm even agnostic about being an agnostic. "I'm agnostic," I once said to the college chaplain. "John, you're not only an agnostic," he said. "You're an evangelical agnostic."

Only a year before Jim died, an Athens real estate developer who was a big-game hunter and admirer of Jim's books invited him to go on a safari, and Jim said yes in spite of his failing health, though it was agreed he would not hunt, but only write and take photos. His host later admitted that he had invited Jim because he felt God had prompted him to do so. Once on safari, Jim decided to shoot a trophy kudu, which he did. Jim felt completely at home in Zambia: "[It] held me enthralled for three weeks as I had not been enthralled since childhood when I had no past and the future held no threat."

Several years ago, I was surprised to see the Sitka lecture as the selection of Jim's work offered in the *Georgia Review* tribute volume, along with material from many others, including Sidney Lanier, W. E. B. Du Bois, Carson McCullers, Harry Crews, and Alice Walker. I expected to see one of Jim's few essays that remain uncollected or maybe a tribute piece written by an eminent scholar who would place Georgian James Kilgo in the context of writers he admired.

Yet in spite of my surprise at seeing the symposium talk published for the first time, the centrality of its subject matter—what must one do with the energy remaining in one's life, and what must a person of faith do in the face of sin?—was not lost upon me. The talk was Jim's greatest apology for his central Christian faith and how it squared with the creation, describing how he felt his beliefs did not place him outside the orthodox canon of writing about the natural world. It wasn't until I reread the piece upon publication that I remembered that I was quoted in it; hence, the second encounter, that of the ghost of my own ideas.

Jim's mention of me in the talk isn't something I completely enjoy revisiting, because it reminds me that I have a tendency to fly off the handle sometimes and say things I don't know if I would stand by fifteen minutes later, much less fifteen years. He quoted a conversation we probably had at some point about the eco-theologian Thomas Berry. I feel now that I wasn't fair to Father Berry's ideas, and I was twisting them to my own devices at the moment. Jim said, "Of the work of Thomas Berry, the poet John Lane told me, 'Berry puts God first, and the earth second. People come in third.'" Rather than a fair assessment of Father Berry's work, this sounds now more like my trying to hold my own, spiritually, with Jim, trying to set up for him the idea that I was different spiritually, but confident in my differences, and that I didn't believe, as he did, in what I perceived as the Christian hierarchy of eternal values: God, people, and then the creation. I was no theologian, and at the time I had grasped onto Thomas Berry because his eco-theology offered me an alternative to contemporary Southern church culture for which I had developed a pretty serious adult allergy. I had read Father Berry's *Dream of the Earth* and I found intellectual comfort there, as Jim found in the Bible. Berry's ideas of an "earth community" helped me understand my stance as an environmentalist. I don't believe now that Berry had such a hierarchy. Now I understand more fully that Father Berry believed in the oneness of things—God, people, earth. I'm still glad that my comment prompted Jim to think about things in his talk, but I wish now I could add a footnote to it.

Mirroring but not matching the hierarchy I projected on Father Thomas Berry, I believe the earth itself is paramount over humans and our faiths. It is ground, and we are the figure acting against it. All human faith traditions, ancient and new, are but a palimpsest. I regularly call the bedrock earth "the wild." Wendell Berry, who also shares Kilgo's Christianity, said that all places are either sacred or defiled. This hints at what I believe. What defiles a sacred place is often specific human action, what Wendell and Thomas Berry and Jim Kilgo might call "sin." The deep mystery itself, the pinging sacredness, is always that spiritual bedrock for me.

But isn't there something else? Something harder, deeper, greater than bedrock? Don't I worry about my soul? I haven't worried since high school that my individual soul was at stake. I believe that the soul of this particular planet is contained in wildness and diversity, and these are of primary value. The arc of the universe is long, I'd say (apologies to Dr. King), and it bends toward wildness, or, as Gary Snyder says, "Wild means process...the wildness is the world. And human agency is only a small part of it." The processes of wildness are my scripture, my gospel.

I also believe that the wildness isn't evenly distributed. Here is where some of my New Age thinking seeps up. I believe in friction points in the land where past and present rub up against each other in a palpable way, power spots. What does that make me? Not an atheist. A pantheist maybe? I believe that this—what we are in now (the Was and the Is, as William Faulkner might say), this mortal coil, this here on earth, call it reality—begins in mystery, and if there is an end, it will be as deep a mystery as it was at the beginning. Mystery is at the bottom of my stratified spiritual landscape, and, for me, religious traditions are layered over it, though some are "thicker" deposits than others. In the Sitka talk, Jim said, "I am a storyteller, not a polemicist." Telling stories has always been my primary metal detector as well, and mystery is always one of the pings I'm listening for.

———

In 2003, the spring after Jim died, I was asked to go to Athens to speak at his memorial service on campus at the University of Georgia. The writers—myself, Philip Lee Williams, Terry Kay, Coleman Barks, and several others—were asked to select a passage from *Colors of Africa* to read in remembrance. I chose to read about a bird Jim had seen along a lagoon in Zambia's Luangwa River Valley, a pied kingfisher "patterned black and white," fixing "its dangerous gaze on the depths below." I remembered Jim's startling blue eyes and the way he would fix his gaze upon all, and I saw the bird as a mysterious avatar, reflecting the words personalizing his novel that he once wrote on the title page of my copy, calling me his "brother in words, brother in spirit."

On the way out of the chapel that night, a barred owl settled on a limb of an old oak and didn't stir as we all passed underneath. I stopped and looked up; the bird didn't fly away, but simply stared down at me. I felt that Jim's spirit was there with me in those fixed eyes, undeparted to the heaven he so deeply believed in.

And then, a year or so after Jim died, I was in Athens again for a celebration of the book *Ossabaw* at the university's museum, where they had a small show of Jack Leigh's photos and Alan Campbell's watercolors. I had written the foreword for the *Ossabaw* collection. Jack Leigh had died the week before of cancer (at only fifty-six), leaving only Alan Campbell standing of the three artists represented in

Ossabaw. I drove to Athens and met the university-press crowd, Alan Campbell, and Jim's widow Jane Kilgo for brunch. Afterward, Jane asked us if we wanted to go over to the house to "see Jim's kudu."

We went to Jim and Jane's house, where they had lived since 1990, and it was like walking back into Jim's life. Even though I had stayed at the house twice, I'd never really looked around at the outward signs of Jim's writing and faith. The kudu was mounted low on a wall in an enclosed side porch. The antelope head was huge, horns piercing upward, and cocked so that one eye was looking to the side. I saw the folds in the skin of the neck and the marks on its shoulder that the hunting guide had told Jim were lion scratches.

Downstairs was one room where Jim worked. There was a small desk off to the side. The bookshelves were full of volumes by his favorite writers, many of them signed. There were Bible verses penciled on the wall next to the desk that Jane said he wrote up there during his illness. An Alan Campbell watercolor of a cheetah hung behind the desk surrounded by Bible verses on Post-it notes that people left on Jim's hospital door at the end. In the next room, one of Jim's bird carvings, a woodcock, sat on a nest in a glass box.

After that, we went upstairs to Jim's study. It was a long, narrow room filled with papers and copies of posters and pictures of him with other authors, including Shelby Foote. Jane apologized and said that though Jim was neat and careful with his writing, he did not work hard at order in his study. You could see next to his desk and computer the last research books for the Africa material. There was

also a place on the wall where he taped pages with the outline of his only novel, *Daughter of My People*. Quite moving, all this, and caught in amber just as he left it.

Later, at the museum, I read a little of my foreword
from *Ossabaw*, and Alan Campbell talked about the col-
laboration between him, Jack Leigh, and Jim, and then
they played a recording of Jim reading his Ossabaw essay
accompanied by slides of Jack's photos of the island. What
Jim read was the early draft of the Ossabaw essay. It had
been recorded at the Southern Nature Conference in Athens several springs before and broadcast on public radio. It
was different than what he prepared for final publication
in *Ossabaw*, and I would argue, so much more interesting
for the things I'm looking for—signs of the deep mystery.
Jim struggled in this early draft with a particular moment
he had when he encountered a little mangalitza pig on the
island, the possible DNA remnant of the original pig population left on Ossabaw by the Spanish. "I stepped forward
for a closer look, but just as an image reflected on water is
broken into a thousand flakes by a sudden gust, so the silver pig disintegrated in a shaft of light and shadow that
rustled the undergrowth." At this point in the recording,
he called the pig's color "numinous" and then jumped to
"numen" as he tried to pin down whether the pig was the
god of the island or not, and whether he should "follow
those pigs wherever they took me." He wondered if the
little pig *was* a god. "A" god; not "the" God. It's a deeply
neo-pagan moment with powerful possibilities of transfor-
mation.

In Jim's published essay, the little mangalitza pig is
still encountered, but the encounter with the numen is

removed. The wild pig is bled of its divinity in the published version. Its color is "an illusion of silver...simply a trick of sunlight," merely a "pig painted silver by the sun."

Maybe this is an insight into why Jim did not finish the longer book about Ossabaw, and maybe not. If he had written a book that proceeded out of that encounter with the numen, I imagine it could have had a particularly pagan tilt to it, maybe even leaving little room for Christ on this wilderness island full of pagan gods. But maybe not. Who knows what Jim would have done with the material? All we know is what he did. The final revised essay he published posthumously in *Ossabaw* sounds more like Jim's earlier journalistic work describing Groton plantation and captured in the spiritual lyricism of *Colors of Africa*.

But why should he have followed this numen? He was a believer looking for transcendence. I believe all his hunts, near his end, had a clear, singular quarry—his final relationship to Christ. My quarry is still more like that Jim's fleeting pig sighting in the Ossabaw woods—"broken into a thousand flakes," a presence "disintegrated in a shift of light and shadow that rustled the undergrowth." What will I do and say when I am looking into the final abyss? Build a medicine wheel? Sit in meditative posture? Read fairy tales? I don't know yet what Jim faced, but I know I, too— as all sentient beings must—will face the abyss someday.

Looking back now, I wonder if it was hard for Jim to be on Ossabaw with so many of his nature-writing friends who were not practicing Christians, especially at the end with his illness. Like all humans, Jim wrapped himself in the mantle of his faith at the end—the trip to Africa and those Bible verses on the wall. And yet in his house were all the literary books he loved sharing space with the Bible—books by all of us, his friends, the writers.

I was deeply moved by the walk back through Jim's home that afternoon. Even if I could not reconcile our gods, I could warm once more at the altar of our friendship, and that visit to his home allowed me to do so. At the end of the Sitka talk, Jim took a reconciling tone. He must have known that many of those listening to him that night in Alaska weren't Christian in any traditional sense. He must have known that if what he offered sounded too much like preaching that his listeners would think a Southern TV evangelist was looming before them. Many of them were like me—interested more in wildness than traditional "protestant" forms of worship and holiness. Jim said, in the final paragraph of his Sitka talk, "Please don't misunderstand me. I am not saying that the salvation of the earth depends on the conversion of the world to Christianity," and then asserted his belief that "if Christianity is right in its belief in the resurrection of Jesus from the dead, as I believe it is, then this beautiful blue-green planet as well as those who live on it can take comfort in the redemptive power of God to heal, to make whole, and to give new life." Then he concluded with Gerard Manley Hopkins: "The world is charged with the grandeur of God." Any believer can say amen to that. Call it mystery, call it God, but call it important enough to fight for, and, yes, to save.

Jim's writing life did not end with his Alaska talk. He went to Africa, and his religious perspective changed when he decided to go. In Africa, Jim made direct contact not just with the old gods, but also stayed close to his one "creator God" and found a way for the two ideas to dwell side by side, something I've always struggled to do. Africa and his host's hospitality gave him a chance to hunt for a kudu and, by taking this final trip and testing his faith, to hunt for God at the same time, "to pursue something real, not just a theological idea."

Encountering the two versions of Jim's interpretation of his Ossabaw Island experience, I saw the shadows of his last flirting with what he called, in an earlier essay, "the red gods," and gave me occasion to think about my own spiritual ambitions. Being a believer in mystery, these ambitions are always under question.

Not being a Christian, I may never understand completely what shifted Jim Kilgo's imagination away from the island he had grown to love, a place still in need of a complete story and a strong conservation voice. Was it the pig that convinced him he could only write the island book if, as he said in his Sitka talk, he could "find the literary form that would contain and express a Christian nature writer's experience?" Maybe the wilderness backdrop of Ossabaw offered up too little of the Christian God and too much numen for his quest. Africa and its landscape, in the end, became the center that held a more potent backdrop for his Christian witness than Ossabaw. For Jim, "the world as it is made" drew near him in Africa, and he sang its maker's praises in his final book.

Piedmont Dreams

Much of my life I have worked close to my childhood home here in the Piedmont of South Carolina. Besides teaching thirty-four years at Wofford College, I have written about what's been called nearby nature, rivers, woods, hawks, coyotes. Wofford is a traditional liberal arts college, and most students stay within disciplinary silos. At the end of the 1990s, after twenty years in the English department, I helped build an environmental studies major that was the college's first fully interdisciplinary program.

Barry Lopez visited Wofford College in 2000 and again in 2010, and his time on campus was instrumental to the establishment of the environmental studies major. Both times he rattled our institutional frame, and he helped put things in motion that have altered the ecosystem of the college for what I think will be a very long time.

Barry was my friend and mentor for forty-one years, and yet, as is often the case with friends, we were different but also much alike. I am a lifelong Southern boy; Barry was born in New York, then moved to California, then back to New York, then to university in the Midwest, and finally lived fifty years in Oregon. Barry was widely known for the wisdom he brought back from the faraway. Some might say he made his mark as a traveling literary shaman. The landscape I am associated with is the Carolina piedmont; Barry will be forever associated with the distant Arctic, where he gathered data and registered irreducible magic in the light, ice, animals, and native peoples there.

In 1986, his book *Arctic Dreams* won the National Book Award.

Barry died on Christmas Day 2020 after a long battle with prostate cancer, but his last years were richly productive. He found energy and space to finish his six hundred-page magnum opus, *Horizon*. In *Horizon*, he wrote, "In every culture in which I have encountered formal elders, the people...carry the history of what will work and what won't."

The first time Barry visited Wofford in 2000, we weren't yet thinking about environmental studies. The Hub City Writers Project, a local arts organization I'd co-founded, planned to use his appearance to kick off a week-long interdisciplinary environmental arts festival celebrating Lawson's Fork, our local waterway. Wofford and Hub City would both benefit from his presence in town.

Walking along our local river the first afternoon, we talked about the upcoming festival, and I told him we wanted him to answer the question, "Can stories save a river?" Barry said the answer was yes. Walking along the stream's banks, he showed me how—he reversed my relationship to the living stream. I had called the stream "impaired," compromised by non-point-source pollution like runoff from septic tanks. "John, it's not the river that's impaired," he asserted. "It's our relationship to it.

The next day, a group of us took him on a hike in the mountains, to a magical destination called Big Bradley Falls. Along on the trip were two students, Kristen Hite and Will Garland. Kristin is now an environmental lawyer and is the UN's Special Rapporteur on the Rights of Indigenous Peoples; Will is a high school English teacher who twenty years later still keeps Barry's work on his syllabus. Gerald Thurmond, one of my colleagues, wrote of that day in his journal. He recorded how Barry talked about story and how he said fiction should have the attitude of a dream. In writing fiction, he said, you just make a start and see where it takes you. Gerald had just finished Barry's *River Notes* and said Barry's book was as much like a river as any one he had ever read. Gerald recalled on the hike to the falls that we scrambled down from the old logging road that leads to a small overlook. Below, a hemlock partially obscured Bradley Falls, and Barry identified as ravens two large black birds that were flying below us. I have read enough spiritual ornithology to know the significance of ravens—always gatekeepers to sacred landscapes.

That night, Barry read "The Near Woods," an essay about a black bear living at the edge of the wilderness in Oregon, unwilling to sacrifice the easy access to civilization for deep woods. He also read "Jedidiah Speaks with the River," a short story. I felt the second reading was a gesture toward me and my question from the day before. The story begins with Jedidiah saying to the river, "Good morning. Can you forgive me?"

At a dinner following the reading, Barry told us of his work with E. O. Wilson to help create an interdisciplinary arts/natural history program at Texas Tech University, where he was a visiting scholar once a year. At that point, there was no similar program for students like Will and Kristen at Wofford, where they might study field science and arts and huminites and somehow find a new way of ordering all the information we are awash in through story. That sort of interdisciplinary thinking, he suggested, might work even better at a small liberal arts college where people were closer to community.

I'd first met Barry at the Power of Animals Conference in Port Townsend, Washington, in April of 1979. Presenters that weekend included American environmentalist and deep ecologist Paul Shepard, poet Gary Snyder, ecofeminist Susan Griffin, poet Melinda Mueller, storyteller Howard Norman, and Barry Lopez. There were maybe twenty-five or thirty participants. The conference was the brainchild of poet Sam Hamill, editor of Copper Canyon Press, and I was his right-hand man that weekend. I was the one who drove over to SeaTac airport to pick up participants. I erased the blackboards after the lectures, and I wrote down what was written there in my notebook.

That first meeting between us laid the groundwork of our common love of place. Soon after Port Townsend, in the summer of '79, I was off on a crocodile survey to Central America, and Barry instructed me as to what my role should be as a poet among field scientists—listen, watch, record. But, unlike Barry, my life work did not proceed to focus on faraway landscapes and animals. I fell in love instead with the animals of the nearby more than the charismatic polar bears and sea eagles. There was a real seed of my writing in that moment in Port Townsend, and also a seed as to how I developed my love of the nearby and how I could pass that life on to others through teaching. Barry helped set me on my path as a young writer. A decade later, after a wandering apprenticeship in which I stayed in close contact with him, I found myself back home in Spartanburg at age thirty-three, teaching where I had grown up.

The second time Barry visited Wofford was in 2010. In the intervening decade, we had begun to use the interdisciplinary Texas Tech model to help build an environmental studies program. We had also acquired a field station on Lawson's Fork, and we were figuring out how to make it useful to our community of students, faculty, and staff. The afternoon of his lecture, we took him out to walk with students, tour the new Goodall Environmental Studies Center, and experience the recovering textile-mill site along the river.

How might we use our presence to create a sacramental relationship with the stream? That's what a group of faculty asked Barry at a special breakfast one morning. Some had the idea that we might create a community around an anagama kiln, as Barry had described in his essay "Effleurage: The Stroke of Fire," from his essay collection *About This Life*. Maybe that sort of intentional community created around art could happen at Glendale?

Barry listened and instructed us to think about ceremony. "Animals are parallel cultures," he explained. "You need to consult and incorporate all the nonhuman cultures that are occupants of the place. Story is the bridge. Build the bridge between arts and the landscape."

I realize much of our work since has been focused on ceremony. We have collected study skins from roadkill mammals and tried to give these animals some dignity and use, as Barry had taught in his short book about roadkill, *Appologia*. One class built a labyrinth near the river. We have yet to build the great dragon anagama kiln, but a colleague created a mud pizza oven from nearby earth and stones, and many flaming firings have darkened its interior.

The wood we burn in the oven is deadfall from the grounds. A student constructed a healing poetry garden along the river. Another set of students created a small shack for outreach programs, built from the timber of an old chicken coop and a threshold board pulled out of the creek's flotsam. Inside our environmental center, our guest book is graced with a photo of Barry signing the ledger.

Barry's legacy will continue to show us what works. He lives on in many ways, both visible and invisible, documented and anecdotal. It's still easy to locate and acquire his dozen or so important and beautiful books about landscape and the imagination. If you Google Barry's name, you could spend days sorting through the links—videos, recordings, photos, interviews, tributes—but none of this gets at his living presence, how, shaman-like, he animated space and rearranged perspectives.

Yesterday I walked along the creek near dusk and lay down on the riverbank next to where a beaver has been dismantling a young tulip poplar since late October. I stayed there, listening to the river flow, making my own ceremony.

One of the last times Barry visited Texas Tech, he told my friend Kurt Caswell that after he was gone, if anyone decided to think or speak or write about his life, he hoped they would conclude that his life helped. His life helped immensely here in the Southeastern United States. He helped us establish and clarify our Piedmont Dreams.

Barry forged a language, reverential and deep, and he continued an old monastic method best shown in *Arctic Dreams*: Go into the landscape. Try to understand, but first listen and see. Note your presence so your hard-won lessons can be used by you and others later.

Acknowledgments

"Chronophilia" appeared on Terrain.org; "Encounters of an Animal Kind" appeared as three "Kudzu Telegraph" columns in the *Spartanburg Journal*; "Ant Farm" appeared in *Cutthroat 27* in a special issue coedited by J. Drew Lanham; "James Dickey's Animals" began as a talk for the James Dickey Conference and was later published in *The James Dickey Review*; "The Bear in the Freezer" began as a talk at Goucher College; "Newt Love" first appeared in *Green Letters*; "Throwing Stars" in *South Carolina Wildlife*; "Rare Birds" appeared in *Enthropy*; "Piedmont Dreams" was written at the encouragement of Norman Bissell for the Scottish Ecopoetics Journal *Stravaig*, issue #7.

The title of James Hillman's collected work on animals is called "Animal Presences," and one of the pieces uses the title "Coming into Animal Presences," which I have borrowed for this collection. Hillman's spirit is behind much of this writing. He once told me to pay attention to the "angel aspects" of words. I hope there is a little of that here.

Thanks to all my good friends at Terrain.org. To Drew Lanham for reading and encouraging all things birdy and beastly, and especially for the idea about the Abaco parrots. Thanks, Drew, also for always listening. To Matteo Meschiari and Ann Kilgo Meschiari for reading and encouraging me to finish the Kilgo "Wild God" piece, and to John Kilgo for looking at the final version. To David

Taylor for his ongoing insight and support. To Terry Gifford. To Kurt Caswell for listening and reading. To Jim Warren for reading and his stories about following elk in New Mexico. To Tom Moore Craig (1944–2022) for access to A. C. Moore's letters about evolution. To Ab Abercrombie and David Scott for always taking a poet into the field with them. And as always, to Betsy.

About the Author

John Lane is the author of many books of poetry and prose, two of them, besides this one, specifically about animals. *Coyote Settles the South* was one of four finalists for the John Burroughs Medal in 2016 and named one of the year's "Nature Books of Uncommon Merit" by the Burroughs Society. He also published an almanac following hawks for a year called *Neighborhood Hawks*. As an environmentalist, Lane has been named Upstate Forever's "Clean Water Champion" and "Water Conservationist of the Year" by the South Carolina Wildlife Federation. In 2014, he was inducted into the South Carolina Academy of Authors. With his wife, Betsy Teter, he was one of the cofounders of Spartanburg's Hub City Writers Project. He is emeritus professor of environmental studies at Wofford College and founding director of the college's Goodall Environmental Studies Center.